D.U.I.

Don't Underestimate It!
By: John Wylie

A Scottish immigrant, living the
American dream, nearly loses it all,
in this intriguingly true tale of greed, red tape,
and walking the line of the U.S. court system.

Outskirts Press, Inc.
Denver, Colorado

D.U.I.
Don't Underestimate It!
All Rights Reserved.
Copyright © 2009 John Wylie
V3.0

To contact the author directly please email him at: Pacospain_8@hotmail.com

Outskirts Press, Inc.
http://www.outskirtspress.com

ISBN: 978-1-4327-3644-6

Library of Congress Control Number: 2009929856

Outskirts Press and the "OP" logo are trademarks belonging to Outskirts Press, Inc.

PRINTED IN THE UNITED STATES OF AMERICA

Foreword

I would like to thank my friend Greg Waskowiak for motivating me to start this book and also his "cuzzin" Jimmy Waskowiak who did a terrific job of designing the cover.

I would also like to give a special thanks to Frank Alexander McFarlane (known as Alex in the book text) my friend of 20 years, who's experiences and crazy adventures together with mine have helped make this a truly interesting, sometimes serious, sometimes funny story.

John

Contents

Chapter One

Living the Good Life in the Land of the Free
--- We Shall See?

My name is John Noble Wylie; I am a native of Scotland who immigrated to America 16 years ago in 1991. I lived in Hartford Connecticut for 5 of the 16 years and the last nine years I have spent in a small town called Rocky Mount in North Carolina, 50 miles east of Raleigh.

Seven years ago at the age of 51 I thought I had it made, senior management position in a large international aerospace company. 125,000 dollars/ year salary and travelling frequently on company expenses both in the contiguous united states and many countries overseas. In ten years of traveling I had already accumulated 780,000 frequent flyer miles with one major airline not to mention the other thousands of miles on other airline carriers.

I truly believed I had the world by the ass on a downhill slope, cruising financially, in fact living like a millionaire would like to spend his life, I say it like this because most millionaire's I've ever met hate to spend a penny of their precious fortune. But not me, I spent my own salary freely; I wanted to see everything and experience everything that this Superpower had to offer. I also had a large company expense account that I used to the full, I never held back on that either, I felt that this was part and parcel of the job, customer's had to be wooed and entertained hadn't they? And I was definitely the right guy for that job.

The Aerospace Consortium was owned by 5 international partner companies, U.S.A., U.K., Japan, Germany, and Italy and one of our major customers was located in France, therefore traveling often to these countries was routine for me, business class or first class of course.

I had a young thirty nine years old wife, 12 years my junior, whom I adored, she drove a brand new Audi 1.8T sports car, myself a new Ford 4.6L Thunderbird and if that wasn't enough we lived in a spectacular new house on North green Country Club Golf Course. The house was so big compared to Scottish standards, 3.500 square feet, 5 bedrooms, 3 full en suite bathrooms and a huge games room, where I proudly displayed my Queen Anne antique pool table with the leather pockets. The house was so big that when my brother came over from Scotland on a golfing trip he thought it was actually north green Country Club Clubhouse itself.

As well as having all these material things, my wife and I were madly in love with each other, having known each other eight years and married after living together three years.

I was living the American Dream wasn't I? Or was it really just a dream--- and it wasn't happening after all.

It did, it didn't, it did, it didn't, fuck no, it couldn't really be me, time and time again I said this to myself .

I used to walk around the house in amazement, was this really me, the wee boy who grew up in the 50's in the slums of Glasgow where if you didn't have scars on your face, holes in the soles of your shoes and some of your teeth knocked out you were a woozie for sure or as we say in Scotland a Cissie, local term for a wimp.

So here I was living by own admission in unashamed luxury, excited about it but at the same time almost embarrassed about it, always trying to justify it to myself, maybe my conscious bothered me for living so affluently, I was working class after all, no pedigree at all for such luxurious living.

And boy, I spent it as fast as a I could make it, wining, dining, in the best restaurants, no fast food places for me, exotic vacations, visits to the horse racing tracks, but only the best ones, no donkey tracks for me, Saratoga Springs, Belmont, Gulfstream Park, Delmar, Hollywood Park and finally Louisville Kentucky, the course of all courses.

Such was the extensiveness of my traveling at that time that if you'd asked someone in a bar in Wapakoneta, Ohio, "do you know a guy called John Wylie"? They would probably have said "yes, I know him very well".

Just for the record, Wapakoneta is a tiny little country town in Ohio where Neil Armstrong, the first man on the moon, was born, it's a very small country town about sixty miles north of Dayton, Ohio and they have a dome shaped museum with the Apollo I capsule located on display. I've actually had the pleasure of sitting in it, yeah, the first USA rocket to put man on the moon and I sat in it! It felt really cramped and I couldn't imagine how difficult it must have been to sit there all that time especially if you had an itch or a case of the skitters (Scottish term for the shits or runs)! oooh!

I happened to be in Wapakoneta on a company visit to one of our suppliers who was located in the next town, Lima, it was the middle of January and just after I'd arrived the snow got so cumulous that we couldn't get out the hotel for 2 days solid, so naturally being Scottish my time was mostly spent in the bar and that was when the manager called over to me "hey John are you trying to set a record?" I guess my constant presence at the bar was noticed and the colossal bar tab was too! So, if you're ever in Wapakoneta, just ask for me, they'll still remember after all these years.

My wife and I first met on vacation in Florida, New Smyrna Beach to be precise, in a bar of course where happy hour was loud and everybody was being what they should be "happy".

I was minding my own business at the bar watching these bikini clad party girls doing their partying when a woman called Nellie heard my Scottish accent and asked me to dance. Little did I know at that time that this was to be the embryonic start of my American Dream?

Now Nellie looked good for her age .I thought, I was thinking mid-fifties but a well kept one, but then again she oozed of wealth and the Botox, and the tummy tucks that go along with wealth, and the facelifts and the removed eye bags that go the same way.

And I was right, Nellie was in fact a multi millionaire who was actually in her sixties, she owned two Naval Training Academies and possessed wads of stock that her deceased husband had wisely invested for her.

Nellie was coming on strong to me, but in the background I could see a younger blue-eyed blonde who caught my attention so that's whom I focused my chat line patter on, the line I used normally with great success was " do you have any Scottish in you? " (Most Americans like to think they have Scottish or Irish heritage and a lot of them do) She replied "no" and I was right in there in a flash, I quickly retorted

"Would you like some" corny approach don't you think, but somehow it worked, it always gave me a good introduction to women. I soon found out that my new found love was called Tammy and she was on vacation from the town of Dan forth, Maine, another tiny wee town in Northern Maine where a good fart on a windy day would have blown it off the map! Dan forth is about two hours north of Bangor and there are more moose's and deer than there are townsfolk, and you're either a lumberjack or a lumberjack or a lumberjack's wife and that's what she was her ex husband was indeed a lumberjack.

Tammy had been very few places outside of the borders of Maine, her annual pilgrimage to New Smyrna Beach Florida in the cold Maine winter being the highlight of her simple little life.

Tammy was a very quiet, reserved and private person always very calm even in the face of adversity. I was exactly the opposite, hyperactive, gregarious, sometimes outrageous, a shocker, always happy to be the center of attraction. I had to be on the go 24/7, sleep for me was something that you reluctantly had to do, if I could have got away with it I wouldn't have slept at all.

But they say that opposite's attract and attract we did, three years after meeting in New Smyrna Beach we were married.

Suddenly the woman who had once picked and packed potatoes for a living (sorry I forgot to mention that Maine's second occupation to lumberjacking was potato picking) and who ate deer meat and moose meat night after night,was catapulted into a millionaire existence traveling with me to Japan,China, Germany, France, Italy, England and Scotland.

She couldn't believe it, experiencing the different international cultures, the high class cuisines instead of fast food restaurants and of course I liked gambling, so there were the racetrack visits and the multiple trips to Vegas. Life was good,we were living lavishly and I couldn't help thinking about some of these phrases that usually come from poor folks "money isn't everything" at this point in my life I was thinking "you could have fooled me" as I sat once again in my first class seat heading to Vegas.

Out of all the high living we did over a period of seven years together, the highlight that we remember most was the night we had dinner in the Ritz Carlton Hotel in their French restaurant in Atlanta. This was one night of pure extravagance I will never forget but then again some people must live like this or there would be no Ritz Carlton (this is my justification for going there coming out).

This is how it happened--------we were on a business trip to a conference in Atlanta staying at the Marriott hotel which in itself is luxurious by any standards, but rather than stay there the whole night we decided to take a walk downtown in the late afternoon /early evening.

I'd heard of the Ritz Carlton in London and knew that you almost had to be Royalty not only to get in through the doormen but also to afford the prices, but as we passed it by, we thought to ourselves "let's go in and at least have one drink just as an experience" The lure was too strong and in we went. We entered the revolving door with some intimidation as the doorman with his gold braided cap and his long v-shaped coat (we call it a ' claw hammered jacket' in Scotland, like a carpenters hammer) hanging smartly down to his ankles.

"Welcome to the Atlanta Ritz Carlton", says the doorman "let me know if there is anything I can do for you during your stay here". We were surprised at that point that us noticeably working class folks even got in the door!

We headed straight to the bar which was very old fashioned looking, made me think of a 1930's movie, so much so that I was half expecting to meet Marlene Dietrich at the bar. The antique couches and chairs, the fans and lamps were just sheer opulence and I couldn't wait to get my working class ass sat on them, and sat on them we did as we called the aproned waiter over for our first drink. Now I knew this was not the kind of establishment where you ask for just an ordinary drink, like a pint of lager or a black and tan, no, that would give the show away, wouldn't it "a glass of Pimm's number 5 please and a vodka spitzer for the wife please", I asked "Your drinks will be with you shortly Sir, replied the waiter", the game was on, we were actually in the real Ritz. It was elegant and impressive and impressive it should have been for the first two drinks came to nineteen dollars plus tip (remember this was year 2001), but that was only a sign of things to come. I was on company expenses anyway, so I just brushed it off as routine business expenses. But expenses can only be stretched to a certain limit and as the night went on I began to realize that I was indeed out of my depth, and getting deeper by the moment.

The fatal mistake was just about to be made as I gulped down my last Pimms' number 5, "can we have the menu for the French restaurant please" I had taken French in my schooldays and felt confident that I could at least have some basic understanding of what was on offer assuming that the menu did not have English in parenthesis.

The French waiter lead us to the main restaurant which was spectacular and the menu was soon in our hands, as I was trying to read it the waiter beckoned to me that I was reading it upside down, so the command of the French language that I thought I had, was non existent, I realized then that I had certain French limitations like "Je Ma'appel Jean" (my name is John for those that don't know basic French) and so on.

I would have to ask the waiter the translation of each dish on the menu and he duly obliged with a little snicker which could only be expected because he could see that I had started out cockily.

The other thing that struck me about the menu, there were no prices, which immediately signaled to me that if you eat here you should not be doing so if you're worried about cost.

"Tonight, Monsieur, we have a grande special, it's an around the world 7 course dinner, each food portion is served from a different country along with the country of origin's fine wine. Without hesitation and regard to cost I was suckered right into this, who the hell had ever heard of an around the world dinner before?, only the Ritz I thought to myself.

The menu started with caviar from Russia, escargot from France, Kobe beef from Japan, Mussels from New Zealand, and the remaining courses I can't remember

With each glass of wine poured, the wine waiter would give a detailed account of it's origin," this wine is a blend of ----- made in the valleys of the French Pyrenees, this Rieslings is from the valleys of Rudesheim in Germany, this wine is from-----. During this altercation with the waiter my wife innocently asked, "Is there a test on this at the end of the night"?

Once we had gorged ourselves on the "Around the World" dinner and the seven glasses of wine from each country I was glad we were schnockered because the bill came next, they should have brought smelling salts along with it, because I nearly passed out when I saw it, $468 plus tip, total $563. Now, I had wined and dined in some of the best restaurants in America including the Winston Churchill restaurant on the Queen Mary luxury liner berthed in Long Beach California but this was the biggest bill I'd ever experienced for two dinners. Not content with all this I proceeded to casually tell the French waiter that I really loved their antique cutlery and would like to buy the table set as a souvenir. "How much will it cost to purchase" I asked. He seemed to be taken aback by this request but politely said he would find out if it was even possible, and if it was he would name the price.

After about ten minutes, the waiter returned to the table and without any hesitation said "you can have the cutlery set for $200" "Done Deal" I said, and at that we shook hands the cutlery was now ours.

The Ritz was a wonderful experience, a wonderful experience, and I'll never forget it but it's clear now that the big dogs live in a world of their own, you know that saying "the big dog's eat the little dogs", I felt like a little Chihuahua as we headed out the restaurant and back to the real world

So how did I make it to America and reach such dizzy heights in the first place? It's a long story that spans fifteen years traveling on business back and forth from Scotland to America and since it's over such a long period in time (this could be a book in itself) I'll try to keep it short.

At the age of seventeen I graduated from Grammar School (equivalent of American high school) with good grades in Science, Math, and Physics and was considered by the school career counselors as an ideal candidate for a career in Mechanical Engineering.

Within four weeks of graduating I had secured a job as a technical apprentice with one of the most prestigious companies in the world, renowned for being the manufacturer of hand made luxury cars for the rich and famous, but also renowned to a lesser degree in the Aerospace Industry for their advanced technology jet engines, powering all types of military and commercial aircraft throughout the world.

I was so excited when I came home and told my parents that I had got this job, they were ecstatic, just as I was, for this was in the 60's when a plumber,carpenter or electrician was regarded as a great trade in this predominantly working class neighborhood. A technical apprentice with this famous company was a level above that.

As well as learning the basics of shop floor engineering in my four years as an apprentice, the company sponsored me for a Bachelor of Science in Mechanical Engineering at Glasgow College of Technology in Scotland and I successfully graduated at the age of 23 and was on my way to a career in engineering and ultimately, through time, into Engineering Management.

At the age of 35 the company put the gun at my head and mandated that if I wanted to go any higher in the management structure I would have to complete an MBA course, so off to college I went again, no hesitation had to do it or my career would stall.

After three years of hard work with my MBA degree in my hand I had Grandiose ambitions about my career prospects.

The college had given me a Pass with Distinction which is the highest you can get and nominated me for the Sir Henry Fylde award which is a very prestigious award for academic achievement. My papers were sent to London for adjudication by a panel but I was to learn later that the Sir Henry Fylde award went to an Englishman and not me. I was pissed off but still flattered that I'd even been considered in the first place.

Okay, back to reality I thought, but our ambitions were running high very high and now that I had my MBA, that I'd worked so hard for, there was no stopping me I was heading for the top, no exceptions or excuses.

But life can dish out some cruel blows, sometimes unexpectedly, especially when you seem to be in that "too big for your boots scenario" and that's what happened to me.

At the graduation night out with my fellow graduates we sat in the bar discussing our promotional prospects, I could move into this position or that position or this executive position in three years time blah-blah blah, all big talk.

But during all this big talk Mother Nature had a big talk surprise on its way for me, didn't she?

As we were in this frenzy of promotional discussion I stepped up to the bar and ordered a round of drinks, put the six of them on the tray to take them back to the table, and as I turned around I felt a big fart coming on and innocently cut loose only to find in a nano –second that I had farted and followed through, yes I had shit my pants, the big executive talk and promotional ambitions were now the last thing on my mind. How could I explain this when I got to the table, cause I was already half way there and clean up was the only thing on my mind. As the smell was permeating through the air and in my nostrils and I wondered if anyone else could smell it, oh no maybe Scott and Andy and the other guys or even worse the only lady of the group, Anna, can smell my shitty load as I one by one hand over their drinks. My only thought was to exit gracefully as if nothing had happened and luckily for me it seemed that I was able to keep my little secret to myself.

I felt embarrassed and humiliated as I flushed my underpants down the toilet but my best suit pants were also affected so there was no way I could continue the night. I made an excuse at the table leaving my ambitions behind and headed to the cab stand outside the bar. As I sat in the cab on the 30 minute ride home in my semi stinking state I cursed and laughed at the same time thinking to myself "happens to the best of us, even Royalty, Presidents, Priests, Nuns, Prime Ministers, Actresses, all must have done it at one time ". These thoughts comforted me and I was back on track the next day with my promotional aspirations intact as if it never happened.

Shit or no shit pants I still had a clear vision of making it to the top and I had made my mind up that this was my main objective beyond anything else.

Within a year of achieving my MBA I was promoted to Manufacturing Engineering Manager in the Scottish facility in Glasgow, but I'd a feeling it wasn't going to end there and I was dead right.

Two years later when our Scottish Facility Director of Operations got promoted to Corporate Board of Directors in England and assumed the responsibility for multiple sites within the organization, he wanted to bring some Scottish colleagues who could support him so to speak with loyalty and protection which is a natural thing to do in these circumstances of moving into unknown territory, especially from Scotland to England where there is a long history of animosity.

There were four of us selected in all, we were later referred to by our English colleagues as the Scottish Mafioso, because our newly promoted director was bringing his bodyguards with him, his Capos, and we were all placed in senior management positions within the Corporate Structure so that we were untouchable and could wield a lot of power. As you can imagine this move was not well received by some existing corporate members, not well at all, but power was power and they had to live with it or get out, and some did, just in time before the axe fell!

After three lucrative years with the Scottish Mafia in England I was then seconded to a Director's position with an Aerospace Consortium located in Hartford Connecticut and this was once again a great deal for me as the mortgage on my house in England would be paid for by the company. I also had an American housing allowance and I was provided a company car. My salary started at

11

$97,500 which was high range in 1991, once again life was good, and the American Dream was in sight or was this just the start of the illusion?

In the time we spent in Connecticut we traveled to different places at every opportunity, nothing was spared and nothing was saved .The Grand Canyon, Yosemite Park, Niagara Falls, The Hoover Dam, Vegas, Smithsonian Institute, Nashville, New Orleans and many more of the finest places America had to offer.

We were in heaven for the next five years and when we counted it up we had visited about 30 different states as well as Canada and Mexico. But you know when everything is going too well , you're always expecting something bad to happen like that old saying" all good things must come to an end" and by God it did for us, the big ball of Elephant's shit was heading over the hill straight at us . Read on------

Chapter Two

The Scottish Way

I n Scotland the legal age for drinking is 18 years old but in the fifties when I grew up as a teenager there was no such thing as photo I.D. as there is in America, there was no requirement to carry proof of identity and very few people did except for those that had a drivers license (without photographs). Therefore it was not uncommon for 16 and 17 year olds to be served in a pub, particularly those that were taller or had a heavy growth that made them look older; serving by the bartender was done not by I.D., only by looks.

I started drinking at the age of 17 in the Old Horseshoe bar which has the biggest horseshoe bar in the world at 110ft 6 ins, although I was only 5ft 7 ins tall I had grown a thick moustache and this seemed to be enough to swing it with bartenders.

I remember ordering my first pint of beer, I was so nervous I would be turned away but with the combination of the moustache and my confident demeanor I was served my first pint and was on my way to my drinking career which would span about forty years thereafter.

There are 1,064 pubs in Glasgow which is synonymous with the lifestyle that the Glaswegians are accustomed to, for every restaurant in America, Scotland has an equivalent bar. There are also many restaurants of course for one has to eat after all!

Drinking beer and spirits in these pubs is a way of life, just like the French are renowned for drinking wine, and the Mexicans their tequila, the Scottish drink beer and whisky, and lots of it, fucking lots of it. The pubs are our way of socializing and it is a meeting place for friends, neighbors, travelers, revelers, tourists, in the smaller villages some even take their dog to the pub and let them lie beside the coal fire, a real fire that is.

Many of the pubs are very old fashioned and generate a tremendous social atmosphere, very luring, cozy, friendly, almost addictively so, and the difference between America and Scotland is the pubs are close together so you don't need to drive, cabs are easy to find and the bus and train services are excellent, transportation without a car is not an issue. Not so in the USA, everything's spread out and cabs are expensive and a lot of times don't show up when called---it's a drink driving catcher's dream alright and even in the big cities where you can get a cab, you get a fuckin' Moroccan nutcase driver who scares the shit out of you with his wayward Moroccan nutcase fuckin driving, they're almost like suicide bomber wanna be's.

But it's not all bars in Scotland, we have a lot of privately owned restaurants that are fine dining, gourmet if you will, compared to the multiple chain restaurants in America, been to one Red Lobster or a Chilies or a Ruby Tuesday's you've been to them all in my opinion, they're exactly the same from inside, decor, menu, layout, right down to the lavatory seat dimensions . So I think you will note from these comments that I can't stand fast food restaurants or chain franchises.

Not so in Scotland, we have unique Italian restaurants (not Olive Garden's, I mean real privately owned Italian restaurants like The Piccolo Mondo, La Fiorentina, The L'Ariosta-----etc.) where fine dining is the norm, portion size, flavor and meal presentation are more important than volume which somehow Americans seem to have embraced as the number one reason for eating out, or should I say that "gorging out" would be more appropriate to describe it, I have been in the all you can eat restaurants in America where it's almost revolting to see so many already obese people and their obese children eat plate after plate with huge piles of food on each one of them.

Don't get me wrong I'm not trying to knock the American way of life cause there's Pro's and Con's in every country and I wouldn't have stayed 16 years in America if I hadn't enjoyed it so much, it definitely is the Land of Opportunity for those that want to work hard and if you succeed you can have a phenomenal lifestyle but over eating is definitely a big issue and when I go back to Scotland I'm tickled by the fact that you see very, very few fat people. And it's interesting because when I tell my American friends about this, they think that there's no fat people because there's a scarcity of food, they think we're still in the potato famine years of 1730! How naive! We have plenty of food but we don't want to look in the mirror and see a beached whale looking back at us.

Given the background that you've already read up to this point, it would come as no surprise to you that I have spent almost 30 years bar and restaurant hopping and, looking back I can hardly remember a night when I was not in the bar or having a drink at home (usually the former though), now I don't mean plastered every night, usually mid-week I would have several pints and then as we headed towards the weekend I would get a bit more sporty and have double digit beers plus a few nips (shots of whisky just for good measure---a night cap you know what I mean). But I wasn't alone, the bars in Scotland are absolutely heaving at the weekends so I wasn't the odd man out by any means.

This was our way of life, for any man that didn't drink was labeled a cissie, it was almost like a show of manliness to drink big and drink big we did.

So the point is, I was used to drinking heavily, I could drink with the best of them and put them under the table even though I was only 5 ft 7in tall and weighed 160 lbs. Some said that my body was an engine that ran on alcohol, an alcohol converter; such was my reputation and prowess as a drinker. Very rarely could I not hold a sensible conversation, no matter how many drinks I'd had.

The whole point about explaining all this is that drinking heavily in Scotland is an accepted practice, some bars will even still serve you when you're lying down on the floor and no-one will blink an eyelid! Slight exaggeration but do you get my drift? For every restaurant in America, pro rata, we have a bar, so right there you can see a big difference in social culture.

But Scotland is not all about bars or bagpipes, just like America is not all about eating out. Scotland is a haven for outdoor sports, soccer is the number one sport, followed by golf, rugby, fishing, hunting, hiking, skiing, and Glasgow the city that I lived in is famous for it's artists, both the canvas type and the actors type, although I would have to admit that the most famous Scottish actor of all time, Sean Connery was born in Edinburgh Scotland not Glasgow and started off his career as a truck driver there. Can you imagine a meager truck driver turned superstar?

But back to the 60's when I was a teenager, Glasgow was ravaged by gangs, not quite like Los Angeles is today but still a mean old city where you had to be very careful where you went, walk into the wrong district at the wrong time of night and you might never be seen again. In the dance clubs, the bouncers searched you for knives and if you didn't have one they gave you one! Then there was the famous gangster of all, at that time, his name was Jimmy Boyle and he was a money lending shark and for those that didn't pay on time the consequences were severe, he finally got convicted of nailing his reneging clients to the floor just like Jesus on the cross and received life imprisonment in the toughest prison in Scotland, Barlinnie prison.

Jimmy Boyle was so notorious that when he finally faced imprisonment, he was a target for both warden abuse and inmate abuse, they were always allegedly beating the hell out of him until he decided enough was enough and the only way he could protect himself was to cover his whole naked body and his cell in his own excrement---and it worked, who wants to deal with a shitty ass everyday! He did this for a while until it went to the media and the beatings stopped and he was put in a special project section for lifers. But as I was to find out later, criminals can have incredible talent and Jimmy Boyle showed this with his ability in the special project section to produce wonderful sculptures that just blew everybody away, including his psychiatrist who happened to be the daughter of an English Lord, she ended up falling in love with Jimmy and marrying him in prison. Somehow after this he was on his way to an early freedom ---can you imagine? And became a reformed man and a famous sculptor with his exhibits displayed throughout Scotland and Europe.

The gang era lasted about 5 years until the authorities really cracked down and eradicated them by the early seventies, the streets were safe to walk again and Glasgow was starting to take pride in its new image. So much so that in 2002, Glasgow was awarded the 'European City of Culture" award, the local standing joke was "it's the only place where you get mugged standing in line for the Opera"

Scotland has a plethora of history, from the elegant castles that housed the kings and gentry, to the famous Renee Mackintosh architecture that adorns the bigger cities and the steeple spired churches that are countrywide whether in the big cities or the tiniest wee village, there's always a church right in the middle of it. It's fascinating for me to look up at these buildings and admire the detail involved in the construction and you try to imagine how it was possible in these days of the sixteenth century to have such specialized, individually talented craftsmen.

Back to the difference in socializing culture-------

I really didn't notice the difference between America and Scotland when I first came to America in the mid –seventies, I saw a lot of people partying in the hotels and drinking and driving and I thought it was just like home. So, when I arrived for what I thought was a 5 year stint in America in 1991, I continued to do what I did back home. I had never been stopped by the police before for drink driving in Scotland in over 20 years of driving and took pride in myself that I had never had an accident since I was seventeen and that record still stands at today's date at age 58, yes do you believe, 41 years without an accident.

I was of the mindset therefore that I was a very safe driver and was even more cautious when I was drinking, but I later found out that track records don't count when you fuck up in America, the sentence is still dealt out with the same brutality.

Until my first DUI in America I had never been stopped by the police for any reason, I never broke the speed limit and I always had my car inspections and insurance documents up to date.

But no matter what country you're in, every law abiding citizen fears the flashing blue lights behind them, don't they?

Even if you're completely sober your immediate thoughts are that you've done something wrong and panic sets in with your adrenalin pumping like an over speeding train that can't be stopped . Now that's when you're sober. Even if you've only had a few beers there is a multiplication panic factor and you say to yourself, fucksake, I'm done for now I know I shouldn't have had them 4 beers, or 5 or 6 or 7 whatever. But you still manage to compose yourself, don't you, stay confident you say to yourself, clear and convincing with your words don't slur or you're right fucked. Then the blue lights flash by you and you breathe a sigh of relief, some other poor bastard's gonna get it, not you this time.

But as you read on you'll see that my turn was due, it happened in a flash, a blue flash, my immaculate driving record was gone just like that, it's amazing that it took 30 years for it but when it happened it definitely was a sobering thought.

Chapter Three
The First D.U.I.

My first DUI occurred in Ohio, just outside of Cincinnati in a little town in the middle of nowhere called Fairborn, more like 'bumb fuck Egypt'. It was 2 weeks before Christmas, and I was on a business trip with a colleague who joined me from Indiana. Before he arrived I checked the town out and I thought maybe that they had all been gassed by sarin poison, the same stuff that the terrorist cult had used in the subways of Japan several years ago. Cause there was no one around, and everything looked 'wintry', dull and dreary, and I regarded it as a DAT. (Dead Ass Town).

I headed out about 6:30p.m. And hit a couple of bars on the outskirts of Cincinnati about 15 miles away, trying to find out where the action was. The restaurants, bars, nightclubs, strip clubs, etc.... And sure enough, I was directed to a neat pedestrian only area, where the atmosphere was electric, high class, unique restaurants, and (no chains). Fine wine selections, Irish bars, etc. "Just my cup of tea, says I"! This will do me I said, proceeding to the most expensive restaurant, since I was on company expenses; I wasn't worried about the cost.

After dinner that was washed down with a few glasses full of pussy or maybe it was Pouisse Fouillet, the fine French wine I can't remember, I headed to the Irish bar about 200 yards down the street, and I could hear the live Irish music blasting right out into the street. My step quickened as I got closer to the band, stepping in tune to the Irish Rover rebel song.

As usual, as soon as I talked to the bartender, my Scottish brogue caught the attention of some college kids and before I knew it, I was deep in conversation about the Scottish way of life. As the night went on, there was one woman who was about 23. She was startlingly good looking but smashed drunk, but she certainly caught my attention. She started talking hard core sex to me. Now start talking sex to me when I'm in a strange place, you'd better brace yourself. One slip of the tongue, and it's too late...I'm coming' on in!

My ego was hurt pretty bad though at the end of the night when she said she really enjoyed my company, and then proceeded to give me her mother's phone number, thinking that we would be a super match. Somehow I kept thinking I would be a fucking match alright--- with her. Anyway, as she disappeared into the horizon, I comforted myself; at least she spent a couple of hours talking to me, too bad she sobered up at the end of the night!

Right there I should have known It was going to be a bad, bad night, because, being unfamiliar with the highway system of Cincinnati, which is different from anything I had ever seen before, screwed up I would say would be an understatement. I have driven all over the United States and never seen anything like it, because even sober and in daylight, I got lost 3 times and was headed in the wrong direction, taking me thirty miles out of my way. That was a bad omen, right there, and it crossed my mind that I should return to the little dead ass town (DAT), put my feet up in the little dead ass hotel room and call it a day, but no, the lure of the nightlife in Cincinnati was too strong. There might be some unexpected pussy coming my way, and I'll take it easy on the alcohol, no sweat Cincinnati...You're just about to get a Scottish visitor and a wild one at that.
Now if the road to Cincinnati was screwed up, the return journey in

the dark felt like being a helpless animal in a maze with no one to rescue you. Ever taken the same road several times, and instead of going forward, you end up in the same place time and time again?, in the middle of nowhere, with disorientation setting in, such that a fucking GPS system wouldn't get you out, then frustration sets in, I would love to get the stupid bastard who designed this system, I said to myself, I would love to get him in a dark alley, and get revenge for the stress he's put me through, he must have cheated in architectural college to design a fucked up system like this. So I'm still lost. I think to myself "I'll give it one more try and if I end up in the same place again, I'll stay in the first hotel I see, even though I'm booked into the dead ass town Ritz Carlton ha ha (Motel 6).

Unfortunately for me, I find the right highway ahead, and soon I could see the sign that said DATA (Dead Ass Town Ahead), but I was grateful to see this sign. I had made it to the finishing line I thought. I'm safe, I'm home, and then fuck me! Just as I was feeling relieved, out of the blue as they say, came the blues. Blue flashing lights that is. Can't be for me, I said, for I have done nothing wrong, but the flashing lights continued, and the stark reality set in. I was indeed being stopped by the law.

Being stopped was bad enough, but the cop also played a dirty trick on me. Instead of coming to the driver's window, which I expected, he came to the passengers side, and I wasn't ready for this , it was a rental car and I wasn't familiar with the controls. When he knocked on the window, I panicked, and couldn't find the passenger side window to roll it down. "Bad Start'", I said to myself. "He already has a perception that I must be impaired since I can't even open the window. Because of this, he came around to the driver side, and asked me to step out of the car, which I did willingly.

In Scotland, we don't' have a sobriety test, it's a breathalyzer on the spot and that's it, and although I heard people talking about walking the white line, I really did think it was a joke, but suddenly on that night, it dawned on me, that this was for real. He put down the white tape. It was about 4 inches wide and eight feet long, and he asked me to walk one foot in front of the other. I was shaken at the thought of this, and to me, who was totally unfamiliar with this sobriety test, and already knowing that I was over the limit, walking the white line felt like being a tight rope walker crossing a ravine with a 3000 foot drop! The only difference was he would have a balancing pole, and I didn't.

Needless to say, I failed the first part of the test, stumbling about the half way mark after a good start. I do think I would have failed this test even if I was completely sober because I had damaged both knees as a teenager doing speed skating but I guess physical disabilities don't count when it's 12:00p.m. on a Friday night and you have an aggressive officer moving in for an easy kill, so I kept my disabilities to myself, hoping that my polite demeanor and sensible conversation with the officer might just get me through it.

Not so, the next test I thought was stupid. Why would he ask me to touch my nose? (With the size of my nose, how could I possibly miss?) But touch my nose I did, easily of course, and as I was doing this, he was dangling a flashlight in my eyes, slowly moving it left to right or right to left. "Follow the torch back and forth" he said. Well at least I won't flunk this test I said to myself, piece of cake this is, just keep your eyes completely on that little torch light and you'll ace it. I later found out that this test is a bit more scientific then it looks, because it's a proven fact that a certain amount of alcohol intake can cause the pupils of your eyes to oscillate, and that was what the cop was looking for, and it seems that I obliged.

The numbers test was next. Count back from 10,030 to 10,001, but since I was good at math at school, I found this test no problem even although it was ass end backwards and I breezed right through it without as much as a stammer. Two out of three I thought, surely that little stumble on the white line would be overlooked like the ice skater who stumbles on the first jump and then makes a spectacular recovery to the applause of the judges. I thought I had done the same, particularly with doing so well on the numbers question which was a real tongue tester. **Fucking wrong again!**

Next thing I know I've got the handcuffs on me and told that I would be subjected to a breathalyzer test, and if positive, my rental car would be towed to the nearest garage at my expense. Now it was really happening, **The Night You All Dread** had descended upon me, and it was to be the start of a downturn in my life that I would rather forget about.

There was one more little twist to this, nothing ever goes smooth for me, so why should this ordeal be any different - it turns out that the breathalyzer in the police station was broken and I would be taken to a local air force base to be breathylyzed and held there until the morning if I failed. And fail I did. I blew me a .17 bat which was .02 over the old limit set several years ago, but .07 over the current limit of .10. I stayed the night in a decent room at the Air Force base and it didn't seem so bad, everyone was friendly towards me and wanted to hear me talk. They liked my accent so much. I suppose I was probably the first live Scotsman that they had ever met in this little mid-west town, so they were intrigued by me, I was like a circus attraction to them.

I appeared in court the next morning for the first time in my life, and I hadn't a clue what to do. My first thought was just plead guilty. (It's your first ever offense, the penalty can't be that bad). A fine, a driving ban, community service. Jail time never crossed my mind. That never happened in Scotland for first offenders. I listened to some of the cases heard before me and was surprised or even shocked by the severity of the sentencing compared to Scottish standards. I realized then that I was out of my depth and almost simultaneously as I was thinking this, an elderly looking, well dressed gentleman approached me and asked me if he could represent me, and at the same time handing me his business card 'Marshall & Marshall' Attorneys at Law.

After a few questions Marshall said that he would deal with my case for a fee of $500, I thought this was expensive at the time but realize now that I got the bargain of a lifetime.

Marshall drove me to the airport and on the way told me he had given up drinking 20 years ago and that all that drinking had done for him was to get him into trouble, and he hadn't missed it since, and he hadn't been in trouble either.

He was leaving me with a message that I should've heeded and continued to warn me about the penalties for getting caught again, not in specific terms but enough to make me realize that it would be no picnic.

But in this case I got off too easy, Marshall called me about 2 months later and told me it was all over, a three months ban, a $500 fine and no jail time, I was so happy I had to sit on my hands to stop myself from clapping, for even although it was my first offence I was still very worried about the outcome.

The worst was over I thought, this can never happen to me again, never, I would rather walk a mile over sharp cobblestones in my bare feet than go through this again -------but never say never---read on and you'll see what I mean.

Chapter Four

The Second D.U.I.

After D.U.I. 1 in Ohio, I never drove my car anywhere at all, except to work and the store and back. My wife became the designated driver, like it or not. I had instilled it into myself that I would never drive again with any alcohol at all in my body and lived up to this commitment up until the second Night you Dread. Up until this day, two years after the event, I'll never figure out why I drove the car that night There were certain circumstances which occurred that night that I could use to mitigate what I did or justify it in my own mind, but all said and done I decided to take a chance and lost the gamble big time like a high roller who knows he's on a losing streak but can't stop.

Another factor was that I had no idea of the severe consequences that were about to be set before me. And my father's words came to me loud and clear, "You can do anything you want, as long as you're prepared to face the consequences". The truth is, I definitely did not know the consequences would be so severe; otherwise I would never have stepped into the car that night. As you read through the second part of this chapter, I will leave it to you to decide whether the consequences I suffered were justified or ridiculously harsh - I think a bit of both, but then again, I'm likely to be biased, aren't I? This is what happened-------

I was called at short notice to a corporate meeting in Phoenix Arizona, due to some problems that had surfaced with a major customer My wife warned me sternly before I left for Arizona, "whatever you do, don't rent a car, do not drink and drive, you've lived in Arizona and you know how tough the D.U.I laws are there". At the time, I nodded in acknowledgement, but I was never one for taking good advice the first time around, was I? So while it was stuck in the back of my mind, I hadn't got the message because the first thing I did at Arizona Airport was to do the bloody thing that she told me not to do - yes, I rented a car.

But like all drunk drivers I had good intentions, didn't I? Just ride the car to the hotel, and to work and back. How can you get into trouble doing that? I said to myself. And until the last night, Friday night no less, I had been on my best behavior, but I was soon to drop my guard, unfortunately for me, I finished work early in the day, and decided to visit old haunts that I used to frequent when I lived there and see if I could bump into anyone I knew to bullshit with. I visited a few bars and really rationed myself on the beer intake with an occasional O'Doul's (non-alcohol beer) thrown in. What a good boy, I thought... I was responsible for once in my life, willpower man you know? Sheer willpower, I could do it! Well it turns out that I couldn't do it! As fate would have it, I did bump into someone I knew, and then we started beer after beer, more beers for the road - you know how that goes? The road is endless.

Worse was to come. Just when I was ready to go back to the hotel at 6:00 p.m. and hang my boots up for the night, my cell phone rings, and it was one of my business colleagues inviting me to his favorite Italian restaurant. "Great says I", I'm never one to turn down an invitation to a night out, but this was to haunt me as one of the biggest mistakes I'd ever made in my life as you will see in the following chapters.

Dinner was arranged for 7:30 p.m. and I arrived promptly to find that the restaurant was backed up real bad, so what did we do? - Yes, we sat at the bar of course, just what I needed, more drinks We sat at the bar, and it seemed we waited for hours on a table, and we were celebrating our business successes and talking about the good times ahead, but the good times were not to be ahead for me, not at all. Bad times unknowingly imminent.

After about 2 hours at the wine bar, at 9:15p.m. To be precise, the matre'de shouted out, "Mr.Wylie, your tables ready!'. By this time, I needed a fucking wheelchair to get me to the table. Now the days drinking total is 10 beers, 5 glasses of wine, and yes you got it, more wine to come at the dinner table. You can't eat Italian pasta without good Chianti, can you? All of a sudden, it was now 11:00 p.m., dinner was finished, and it was time to go. I knew I'd had a snuteful, and thought momentarily about calling a cab, but no, how could I? The hotel was only 3 miles down the road, a five minute straight drive. No problem put it in cruise control and you'll be right there in no time.

Fuckin' wrong again. No sooner had I left the restaurant car park, when I noticed a motor cyclist in my rear view mirror. I thought it may have been one of these Hell's Angels type, riding a Harley, but no such luck for me, it was indeed a Motorcycle Cop, now the blue lights were flashing, and I was once again facing the **Night You Dread.**

This time I was caught red handed like a thief with his hand caught in the cash register or on a security video camera, no excuses, I was well oiled as they say in Scotland (equivalent of shit faced in American terms). I knew the minute I stopped for the blue light I was a goner this time. I knew I was in deep, deep trouble, and I would have difficulty composing myself, even to speak coherently would be a huge effort. As the cop stepped down from his motorcycle, I felt like putting my head in my hands and raising the white flag to surrender, but no, this drunk was going to fight it until the end, but in reality a deep feeling of guilt engulfed me as I was not a man that typically set out to break the law. My parents brought me up to do the right thing. (Even though Old Jack was drunken bastard himself). I always had abided by the rules, but this time I felt I let myself and my parents down badly.

While I was facing the motorcycle cops interrogation, and in a self pity state of mind, a brainwave came over me. I had my Scottish driver's license on me. The car I was driving was a rental car, and therefore I could convince the cop that I was on a business trip from Scotland, and maybe he would have compassion for me, and let me off with a warning. A nice gesture from an American to a Scottish visitor in his country, so I thought. **Fuckin' wrong again!**

This 'brain wave' was to backfire on me through the passage of time, and will live with me forever, as you'll see in the subsequent events that followed, this brain wave precipitated what I believe was a series of events that put me deeper and deeper in trouble. Now the sobriety test. When I asked the cop to stand still while I climbed up his leg, the sobriety test was over. Crawling along the white line wasn't an option, and you can't take the 5th amendment on the 10,030 - 10,001 numbers test, so it was handcuffs again, and heading to jail for another breathalyzer test. I blew a .234 Breath Alcohol Test, which was embarrassing, because usually I don't even drink as much as that when I'm not driving, but I felt nothing but shame and remorse.

When the reading printed out on the ticker tape from the machine, this was when reality set in, as the cop completed the charge paper work; I read the words 'Extreme D.U.I'. A category I didn't even know existed, and the very word 'extreme' indicated to me that the consequences were going to be extreme as well, and extreme they were.

I had handed the cop my Scottish driver's license and he was completely bamboozled by it, since it was in paper form, no picture ID, and was valid for twenty years, with absolutely no violations recorded on it. After about 30 minutes, he actually managed to get the drivers license right way up, so it became readable to him. Despite my inebriated state, I was hoping against all hope that by giving this license and my Scottish address on it, that they would not be able to trace my first DUI offense in Ohio. "Good thinking wee man, I said to myself, good strategy, still compus mentus eh?" (Latin for maintaining your mental stability, just in case you don't know this term). After 10 glasses of wine, and 10 beers, fooled the fucker I thought, **wrong again!** This was to become my Achilles Heel during the court proceedings that followed and demonstrated to me once again that trying to beat the System is a lost cause. It's too structured and all too powerful as you will see.

After proving positive on the BAT, very positive, (It's a wonder the machine didn't blow to pieces) I was taken to the stinking rotten Maricopa County Jail, and let me assure you that stinking rotten is no exaggeration, stinking rotten it is. If there was a stronger adjective I could think of, it would be more appropriate.

The cell was a typical one you see in the movies, with a solid steel door with no outside windows, and a small 18' by 18' barred port hole from which all you could see was the officers working nightly through the narrow corridors. Nothing else was typical about the cell, for there were 23 Mexicans crammed in it plus myself and one other Caucasian who was a Phoenix local. This cell was built for about 12 people maximum but it was Friday night after all, the biggest DUI night of the week in Phoenix, a gravy night for the police. It was standing room only in the cell with 1 shitter (that didn't have any walls, but plenty of spectators) It was standing room only alright, I was fucking squashed to pieces and it added a whole new meaning to me for "standing room only". In other words, claustrophobia - Can you get excessive or extreme claustrophobia? If you could then this was definitely it. It reminded me of the time in the 60's when college students tried to set the world record for the number of people that could squeeze into a London telephone kiosk The number they eventually managed I can't remember but I remember thinking that it was impossible, the number was so large - maybe the Maricopa County Jail was also trying to set a record.

The stench of human body odor in the cell combined with the shit and urine smell from the only latrine and the one drunk that barfed up on the floor made the conditions unbearable and I would have done anything to get out - sell my house, my toys, my wife, even my Scottish Bagpipes to get out of this bloody misery that had been inflicted upon me. The 10 hours spent there with the sweat pouring out of me, both from the alcohol the evening before and the body heat being generated by the other detainees is something I'll never forget. The stale smell of alcohol breath would have put you off drinking forever.

I had no idea what to do to get out of this living hell cell. I was not familiar with the bail bondsman's process, but after much gesticulating with my hands and pointing at the telephone, one of the Mexicans finally showed me how to work the one and only telephone in the cell and make the one and only telephone call you're allowed to make. What an embarrassment that was, cause you have to call collect only and the recipient only hear 'Will you take a collect call from Maricopa County Jail?' My wife answered the phone and I could sense from the tone of her voice that she was shocked and disgusted with me, particularly since I hadn't heeded to her warning about not driving in Arizona. My cries were desperate. "Get me out of here as soon as you can I said, no matter what the cost, we'll deal with that later"

As it was a Saturday and my wife was also unfamiliar with the bail bondsman process, It took her about 7 hours to make arrangements with the bondsman via credit card, and when he was satisfied I was happy to see the prison officer who escorted me out of the cell from hell leaving 32 Mexicans still in there with their American Dreams shattered! When the turnkey came to let me out it was now 2:00p.m. In the afternoon. I was perspiring profusely and felt filthy and sick at what I had got myself into.

The sense of freedom leaving the building however overwhelmed me with joy and I was still of the frame of mind that by giving my British drivers license that I would go off with a fine and no jail time. **Fuckin' wrong again!** I kinda snickered to myself as I sat in the cab taking me back to the rental car. I thought once again that I had performed a 'Houdini' on the law and the worst part of the ordeal was over, or so I thought. Only the fine ahead of me no sweat to deal with that.

After all I had been in a few scrapes before, but not with the law, and came out of it unscathed, sometimes with flying colors. I remember my sister used to say to me, "If you fell into the River Clyde (a famous river in Scotland), you would come out with a big salmon in your back pocket". This was an indication of always being lucky, for the River Clyde meanders through the center of Glasgow and was one of the biggest ports of entry for merchant ships throughout Scottish history. Now polluted with industrial waste, you have a better chance of catching a tea kettle than a salmon.

So as I was headed to the airport, I thought all the bad stuff was behind me, only the fines to face and I'm home and dry, thank God that's all over with. (Fucking wrong again!) If I had known what was ahead of me I would probably have fled to Scotland right there and then, never to set foot again in the land that the American Homegrowns call ' The Land of the Free' - We shall see if staying put was the right decision as subsequent events unfolded, because my plan with the Scottish drivers license totally backfired on me unexpectedly and the consequences caused me relentless grief for the 1 ¼ years it took to bring the whole matter to a complete conclusion.

This is what happened------.

Anxious to get the problem over and done with, I called the Phoenix County Court and, pretending to be living in England, I asked for the name of the District Attorney who presided over such DUI cases as mine and explained to the clerk of the court that I would like to plead guilty by letter to the charge. Surely after all with me "living in the England". There would be a compromise made and the court would realize that it was not practical to be prosecuted as an American resident and hopefully the sentence would therefore be lighter. Fucking Wrong again, the judicial system is smarter than you think, They've probably seen every trick in the book and now they've got it trick proof.
It turned out that I could not plead guilty by letter alone, rather that I had to attend a network meeting from the England to U.S.A. in the

presence of the English jurisdiction and face the American judge in a video court scenario where my case would be decided upon.

Also, the court documents would have to be notarized by the English local county police and my address and employment verified etc. etc .etc---it soon became clear that if I pursued this pretence of living in England I would be digging the hole deeper and deeper with more charges likely to be pressed if I got found out.

As these court twists against me became more evident I was starting to panic big time and soon had to admit to myself that my Scottish driver's license ploy was a lost cause and that I would have to seek proper legal advice and bite the bullet so to speak.

With great reluctance and disappointment I contacted an attorney in Phoenix and set up a meeting in person to explain my circumstances which had now become so complicated that I was having palpitations on a regular basis and nightmares about how this whole scenario would pan out.

I was convinced I would be convicted of a felony and after spending a 4 months jail sentence in U.S.A. I would be deported back to Scotland. Note also in America, if you get a felony on your record it automatically prohibits you from ever getting a professional position again, it's part of the screening process and your job application is trashed , no negotiation, no compromise, with a felony you're basically done as a professional.

The attorneys as usual were much more optimistic than I was, promising that they could get the charges dropped down from a felony to a misdemeanor this is an old trick by the attorneys to scare you and make you pay more, and more, and more, they drag it out and eventually it seems that they get you where you need to be --- MONEY talks in the American judicial system, it really does.

After 15 months of $500 installments and deliberate postponements of my case so that the attorneys had their money in their pocket, my case was finally heard----can you imagine the stress involved in the monthly payments and worrying about the outcome? My job on the line, marriage ended, the big house gone , everything lost, dreams shattered, I had it all.

After more months of sweating it out the big day finally arrived, I'd never been in a court before, not even jury duty, and I was petrified, when I stood in front of the judge my knees were shaking and I could hardly speak. The judge proceeded to ask me to confirm my name and then strangely enough to me asked if it was correct that I had a degree in Engineering and a degree in Business Studies and I replied "yes" and then he read out the charges, and this is when the attorney took over.

"Mr. Wylie has been a model citizen in the USA except for the two DUI's which he deeply regrets, Mr. Wylie understands the severity of his actions and asks the court to carry out a fair sentence so that he doesn't lose his employment at the same time realizing that the penalty for such actions has to be paid for" "Please also note your honor that Mr. Wylie has had a driver's license for thirty five years without a single accident and with no driving offences other than the prior "DUI"

"Mr. Wylie pleads guilty and is prepared to accept the penal consequences, and has committed himself to never ever breaking the law again".

The Judge then responded "in view of the circumstances that you've presented before me and taking into consideration Mr. Wylie's impeccable background, the court hereby sentences him to thirty days in jail, 1,000 dollars fine and two years probation" The hammer went down and within seconds I was signing the paperwork to acknowledge my sentence.

My first reaction was at least it's not four months in jail but how am I going to take thirty days off work without my company knowing, then as I talked with the attorney he offered me some relief by stating that he would negotiate with the court to have my thirty days in jail spent in North Carolina under a work release program where I would go to work as normal but be back to the jail each night by 6.00 pm and also spend four weekends there. "This is not guaranteed Mr. Wylie, said the attorney, but I am confident that I can make it happen"

My inner thoughts at that time were 'it's about time you earned your $8.500 legal fees ya dirty thieving bastard ye" However, although I had these thoughts in mind I also had to admit to myself that after all said and done the legal representation would be worth it if the work release program was agreed. And luckily enough for me the attorney actually did what he said he could do (which by the way is probably a rare occurrence) he got agreement to the work release program and I felt as if my life had been saved.

As I sat on the five hour plane ride from Phoenix back to North Carolina, I reflected on what could have happened and although I dreaded the prospect of being confined to jail I was grateful that the outcome was more benign than I had expected, all my worries over the previous fourteen months were over, I just had to face up to the fact that I had committed a crime and had to pay for it, and pay for it I did, as you will see, but I wouldn't have missed the experience for anything in the world, as it turned out in the end. It was an experience of a lifetime, never to be forgotten, an adventure from hell but also a blessing in disguise, I could see the other side of life now and was a changed person, for the better. Prison time will do that to you.

Chapter Five

Paying the Penalty- Pay, Pay, and More Pay

I f anyone would have told me that a second DUI would cost me 4 months in jail, deportation, loss of job, loss of house and car, loss of a wife, and 1 million dollars in earnings, I would have considered them insane. This is America, isn't it? The land of the free, where there is a fair justice system, and the penalty fits the crime, doesn't it? I'll let you be the judge for yourself as you read on in this chapter.

Having given my Scottish drivers license when I was arrested, I had no option but to play this game right to the bitter end. In the sober light of day I had worked out a plan that would get me out of this crazy situation, maybe a big fine and slap on the wrist I thought. I started the process by finding out the names of the judges who presided over the DUI cases and through the clerk of the court I found out the court and the judge who would specifically be dealing with my case. With this information I then proceeded to write a letter to the judge as if it came from my address in the U.K. My sister in Scotland typed this letter up for me and mailed it from my Scottish Address on my drivers license.

There was a little white lie in the letter as you can see. I stated that I had never been in any trouble in my life before, except for my DUI in Ohio, which I was hoping would not show up anywhere, but there are more twists and turns in this story than a king cobra snake makes. You see, when I was arrested in Ohio, I had a North Carolina driver's license by the arresting cop, but I resided in Arizona at the time, which really complicated the whole issue. I was told by the lawyer in Ohio that my North Carolina driver's license would be returned to the Department of Motor Vehicles there, and that they may take some action. This never did happen, and I was of the understanding that no action had been taken.

What I wasn't to know at this time was that Ohio actually notified the Arizona DMV and even worse, the letter revoked my driver license privileges. I had no idea that this notification had happened - The letter was to never reach my new address in North Carolina. Not knowing all of this I continued to pursue my plan of answering the DUI charge from Scotland - Then the shit hit the fan during the back and forth correspondence with the Phoenix court house I was told that I would have to make a personal appearance in court in Phoenix, Arizona or arrange a telephone hearing in the presence of the local police authorities. I pursued this telephone hearing and then found out that my residence in Scotland would have to be verified by a notary from a local police office, so slowly and surely I was getting deeper and deeper into a lie that I couldn't get out of which is typical of all lies - not just this one.

I started to feel out of my depth, not knowing the American judicial system, and all I could see was myself being boxed into a corner with no escape route - this is better known as being "totally fucked" in Scotland.

It was at this point that I panicked and decided to hand over my case to a DUI lawyer in Phoenix. which on reflection, may have been a huge mistake because despite all his assurances that he could mitigate the circumstances he actually never achieved much at all, I had to do it all myself

Up to the time that I had engaged a Phoenix lawyer, the DMV

apparently had no knowledge, because they had no license to trace and they certainly had no knowledge that I had recently moved to North Carolina, so I thought that my Scottish Drivers License plan still stood, and the lawyer would soon represent me from Scotland, wouldn't he? Remember, I was trying to present myself as a Scottish tourist with a Scottish Drivers License. Not so, without my permission the lawyer gave the authorities my address in North Carolina, so from my stand point trying to resolve this issue from the 'U.K', he had betrayed me, he had put me in contempt of court, let the cat out of the bag as they say. A huge faux pas, in French this means 'Huge Error'. Now we can debate the reasons he did this, but let's start by quoting the financial agreement with the lawyer, which was, for an ordinary DUI, a flat rate of $3000.00 would be charged with no additional miscellaneous extras - a fixed price.

However, if the case had to go to trial or become a felony the case would be heard in the Superior Court, then the cost for legal representation would be $8500.00. Isn't it strange that lawyers have Extra Sensory Perception (E.S.P.) when it comes to money and we, the poor defendants don't. Of course it came to pass that the revoked driving privileges combined with an extreme DUI constitutes a felony, which, guess what? Now becomes an $8500.00 gravy train for the lawyer - What a coincidence, eh?

This was my first hint that I was about to be financially bled until I could bleed no more, no tourniquet could stop the flow of blood once the piranha lawyers and advocates of the court had caught the smell of it. To make matters worse, during the course of reviewing my Arizona records, it was noted that I had been caught by a camera speeding in a 35 mile an hour zone, and hadn't paid the ticket. This turned out to be an offense committed by my wife at the time when driving the Audi car back from work in Scottsdale Arizona, but since the car was registered in my name the speeding ticket was charged against me. My thoughtful wife had never told me about this ticket. I had absolutely no knowledge of this, until the court records revealed it.

So all in all the odds were beginning to stack up against me, and on paper I looked like a real villain to anyone who didn't know me personally, looking as if I had a total disregard for the law. I cursed the piranha lawyer upside down and inside out and stamped in anger around the house like a child that had taken a tantrum because he couldn't have candy. After all, he was the one who had ratted on me, hadn't he? Why would he have done this? What possible reason could he have had that would justify giving the U.K. driving license game away.

His excuse to me was that he was worried that the American authorities would somehow connect my British, Arizona and North Carolina addresses and would send out a warrant for my arrest, so in his view he was protecting my interest as a good, honest piranha lawyer should do. I think not so in this case. I'm sure he had his eyes on ringing up another $4500.00 in his bank account instead, with his cash register mind. I had no option in my view but to sign up to a payment plan of $500.00 a month for 17 months, and was happy to do so, thinking that for that kind of money, I must be getting Johnny Cochrane's ½ brother, or at least Vincent Bugliosi's 2nd cousin. **Fucking wrong again!**, no matter how many times I called from North Carolina to Arizona, I could not get the same person twice and they kept getting my case mixed up with somebody else's, until eventually I wrote a letter to one of the partners with all of the relevant particulars.

Plea Bargaining looked like my only solution, for the penalty for a felony was 4 months in jail plus deportation. The very thought of this terrified me and my wife at that time. It seemed that everything that we ever worked for in America would be lost because of one night of complete stupidity on my part. I would surely lose my $105,000 a year job, then my house, and the 2 cars. And the other factor was, I had only 8 months to reach 5 years service with the company's vesting program, which would give me $20,000 in matching shares and pension rights. The loss of salary alone projected over my 10 year working life would be $1,000,000 plus the potential loss of 401k savings and matching shares and a pension of at least $2500 / month for life. So the stakes were very high for me. This could be my ruination of all ruination's within a very short period of time.

After about 3 months of waiting and unanswered phone calls, the lawyer in Arizona called me up and said I have good news, and bad news. I said 'ok, let me hear the good news first" "The good news is that the prosecution are willing to downgrade the charge from a felony to a misdemeanor, which takes care of the deportation issue "If it had been a felony a deportation would be automatic...The bad news is they still want to hold you to a 4 month straight jail sentence. At this point he was putting it across as a pretty good deal, maybe as good as I could possibly get, but as anyone could imagine, being a professional person who had never harmed a soul since moving to America, the scale of the whole situation in my opinion had spiraled out of control, and there didn't seem anyway to recover it.

Once again I explained to my lawyer that the offer was totally unacceptable, surely the court would consider my unsoiled background prior to these DUI's and for God sakes show me some mercy. Was this too much to ask, or is one fuck up in your life enough to wipe you out? Yes or no? According to the way the lawyer was talking, the answer was yes, because he kept trying to persuade me to take the 4 months offer in jail as if I was getting a bargain day at Walmart.

Several weeks went by and the only correspondence that I received from the piranha lawyer's office was the past due notices for the $500.00 a month, which I was barely ever late by 3-7 days. I was still being bounced around by different lawyers and each phone call I would make was very seldom returned, but my $500.00 payments had to keep coming in, or they would drop me. So here I was. I was being totally screwed. I thought that they were taking my money without any conscious, and doing nothing at all for me. After about 10 months of agonizing through the stalemate kind of process, I decided that I had to take the initiative myself, otherwise I would run out of time and lose everything I owned and still have the $500.00 a month payment, so I took the bull by the horns, and I finally wrote the following letter to the presiding judge, which I hoped would demonstrate that I was not the criminal that I surely looked like on paper.

I'm glad to have to tell you that this initiative worked, and the plea bargain was that they agreed for me to serve 30 days in a work release program, which enabled me to go to work during the day and jail each night and weekends, and basically save my skin. This was exciting news to me, and I was ecstatic. My company would never know that I got in this mess. It would be work as usual. I would do my 30 days, and in the evenings and weekends, and the ordeal would be over and done with. But somehow the misery of this, was still to hang over me for some more time, like a storm stalled over the east coast that won't shift, and keeps on dumping a ton of rain on you. This case was exactly like that.

No sooner had the lawyer giving me this news, when he started questioning whether if it could be carried out practically - out of state work release was something he said he hadn't dealt with before and it takes an agreement of the receiving state to make it happen, which in my case was North Carolina.

The first phone call made to the Nash County Sheriff's office by the lawyer in Arizona was negatively received, the sheriff did not believe in principle in the work release philosophy and vehemently turned the request down, and I was devastated. The lawyer told me I would have to canvas other prisons in the county or try to change the sheriff's mind. Thankfully, I decided on the latter course of action and was relying on my professionalism and appearance and job position to persuade the sheriff to authorize a work release program.

For those who don't know about work release, you spend the whole weekend in prison and on midweek days you leave at 6:00a.m. and return at 6:00p.m. After about 20 minutes of conversation with the sheriff he recognized my plight and agreed to work release in his jail, provided the correct paperwork was received from Arizona. Needless to say as a date for the start of the prison sentence drew closer, the paperwork from Arizona was not correct and despite repeated phone calls from the head jailer Mr. Langston, the lawyers still managed to screw up the paperwork and the 3 times I went to the jail to start serving my sentence, I was turned away. Mr.

Langston then began to get furious over this and I almost felt he was taking it out on me unjustifiably, and I finally got the message that I would have to intervene myself again when he said to me sternly, "I'll give you one last shot at this and then I'm sending your paperwork back to the judge in Arizona for you to serve your sentence there".

I was panic stricken once again, back to square one, possibly once again losing my job, my house, my pension rights, etc. etc.., all because of a piece of paper that had already cost me $8500.00 in lawyers fees. I eventually resolved the issue by arranging a 3 way conference call so that I would not be the middle man and we would all discuss the requirements at the same time. This worked and I sighed with relief as I entered into the Nash County Jail House on July 6, 2001 for my 30 days punishment. This was it, the real thing at last. It was like a m someone waiting for a major surgery, the waiting and the fear is usually much worse then the surgery itself.

Before authorizing me into his custody, Mr. Langston told me that since it was an out of state case I would have to pay $25.00 per day for my stay in jail in Nash County and if it wasn't paid (cash only) before the day of my release, I would be kept in jail. This came as another shock to me as I had never heard of anyone having to pay for their own stay in jail, that's why we pay taxes after all, isn't it, or is that just my thinking?

In the following chapter, I will cover some of the aspects of the money system in jail which absolutely astounded me. So now as I sat in a jail, I started adding up the cost of this whole episode, and the costs I had to face ahead of me. The table below shows the breakdown of the cost, and I would be happy to know how any ordinary working man in America could get out of this financial quagmire, never mind a poor man, impossible I say, that's why most men in prison have to do more time then necessary and that's why the jail's are so overcrowded. They could never afford the proper cost of their release. Below is the breakdown of my costs:-

Cost Analysis

Bondsman = $1550.00

Drunk Driving School cost = $500.00

Probation Officer Cost = $600.00

Travel Costs to Arizona (3 trips) = $2500.00

Car Insurance Increase = Twice as much as when I arrived in 'The Land of the Free'.

Interstate Probation Paperwork Transfer Cost = $300.00

Attorney's Fee's = $8500.00

Cost of staying in jail = $750.00

Grand Total = $14,700

Cost of living in the Land of the Free! =PRICELESS!

Chapter Six
Nash County Jail

*N*ow, I wasn't expecting a sleep number bed or satin pillow draped in white lace after all, it's jail isn't it? A place where you get punished and returned back to society a better person- ha !ha !ha ! I was not ready for what I was about to experience, never been strip searched before, never had an orange jumpsuit, never had to share a cast iron bunk bed with no pillow and a mattress that is as thin as paper that you could hold up to the light and see through it, and the orange plastic shoes that we probably now call "crocks" were killing me as they were three sizes too big..

The cell was not an individual one, no, it was a huge cell that held about sixty inmates, the most striking thing in entering the cell was the complete lack of privacy and no outside natural light. The majority of the inmates were huge black dudes, I mean so huge that I wondered to myself if they killed the little ones at birth. It was very intimidating.

Okay, I could live with the cast iron bunk bed but open toilets and showers, I mean open, you take a shit and there is another fifty-nine inmates looking at you, same with the showers as you're scrubbing your balls there's another fifty-nine inmates looking at you or are scrubbing theirs, privacy is out of the question.

Okay, I walk into this place completely terrified, never been to prison before so, what's the first thing you think of? I'll tell you what it is, protection, that's what it is, it's called the Macgregor theory in Scotland, I learned it at college, the first thing man thinks about when everything else is lost – yes, you've got it – survival.

So that's what I had to do, I had to find a way to survive this bloody mess and my first thoughts were to pick the biggest black guy I could find and become his best friend and that's exactly what I did. His name was Sommerville and he became my protector, I say for a while because the majority of the guys in there were in and out of jail all the time, Sommerville was no different, Nash County Jail for a short stretch and then off to federal prison for his long stretch, I missed him after his ten days in Nash County Jail and had to work on the next protector.

Okay, so what is jail really like, let me begin with my perception after thirty days in there. There were burglars, car thieves, muggers, child support dodgers, and DUI's like me, the little guy on the prison food chain, you know what I mean? I was at the bottom of the Totem Pole with my little shit DUI but nevertheless, I was in the communal jail along with the rest of them. There were various characters, like "Batman" a six foot five skinny black guy who had huge ears and a long chin that made him look like a bat, hence his nick name, he even had "batman" printed on the back of his drawers, so, evidently he enjoyed his nickname. He was a plumber by trade and a car thief by night, but he also had artistic talent and made jail souvenirs --- he made me a jewelry box from 1200 Jolly Rancher wrappers that took 2 weeks to do, he also made me a heart shaped picture frame out of Jolly Roger wrappers too, same thing, took about 2 weeks of Painstaking detail and monotony to finish it. Just think about it, he had to fold each wrapper 4 ways to get one structural wrapper made, that's 4,800 folds---but he also had plenty of time to do it! I paid him 30 dollars for both and still have them as a jail memoir in my China cabinet in the living room at home.

There were other inmates who had similar artistic talent, one inmate even made a miniature Harley Davidson motor cycle out of bars of soap, pity these artistic types couldn't harness their talent in a more positive way but it seems to me that once you become criminally inclined then you can only think criminally, you can't adjust to normal society rules and principles evidenced by the number of repeat offenders that are in and out of jail on a continuous basis.

Then there was "Cash Money" his nickname stemmed from his reputation as a mugger and house burglar only dealing in cash money, which he had engraved like a tattoo on his arm but it looked as if it had been carved in with a knife rather than by a tattoo artist.

He took great delight in telling his stories of his victims, some of whom were old age pensioners but it didn't matter to him, cash money was cash money.

Now let's talk about the food, if you could describe it as that, my recollection was like eating your granny's slippers and washing it down with the jail juice that tasted like a glass of castor oil, lovely eh? Everything was synthetic, not real food, as we outsiders know it. Now don't let me forget that you get jello along with each course, that puts the icing on the cake, puts the flavor into the slippers and the castor oil.

Here was a man that was used to Gourmet cooking, make top chefs look like a fucking pieman, but no, this was reality this was me and Nash County Jail, no more Gourmet for me, any chance of another jello, please ?

I've always been used to big portions in the U.S. but this was one time I was glad that they were small, the standing joke in jail was that you just get a big enough portion so that you don't faint in front of the judge when you're at trial.

Meals apart, bad ones that they where, let's change the subject to jail entertainment, I can assure you it's not like Elvis's jail house rock, believe me there are no American idols, no Price is Right, no

Evangelists, and no Porn. The entertainment is- wait for it – yes, you can read the bible all day long, not that I am knocking the Holy Bible but after thirty days of Bible thumping I'd had enough

But we did get some TV, not HDTV or Plasma, the twenty year old TV was forty foot up the wall and the inmates used a fishing pole to turn it off and on and to change the channel from black trivia to more black trivia, I wasn't going to be the one to change a channel to CNN's Wolf Blitzer or Lou Dobbs that would be too sensible and dangerous. Then there was the chess and the dominoes and shoot pool, a few beers and some exotic dancers – sorry just dreaming, let's get back to the dominoes and the chess, because that's all it was, no more no less, "that will teach you to get a DUI" I thought as I hopped up and hit my shins again on the cast iron bunk bed. No money exchanged hands at dominoes or chess but when you lost you had to do ten pushups, that was your punishment. I guess if you were a keep-fit fanatic you wouldn't care if you won or lost, would you? I hated the push ups, never was a keep –fit type, the only push ups I was used to was with bad women or good women depending on how you look at it

I guess the biggest impact that prison had on me was the number of repeat offenders, it seems that once you're in the system you can't get out unless you have one thing going for you- can you guess what that is? Yes, you got it, MONEY. The judicial system in America is money motivated just like any other business, it has to make profit and believe me it is big business and everyone gets a piece of the pie, some larger than others.

Jail was a humiliation beyond belief and I hated it at the time but looking back I wouldn't have missed it for anything. What an experience. **Thank you Nash County Jail!**

Chapter Seven

On the Slide

They say that alcoholism sneaks up on you, and sneak up on me it did, very stealthily, I never even saw it coming .I always had the classic aptitude for it—stressful job, highly strung personality that some would describe as hyper active or hyper hyper active perhaps . I was also a workaholic who pushed himself right to the limit searching for success at any cost, pushed the envelope both at work or play or burned the candle at two ends, if there'd been three ends to a candle then I would have burned all three of them.

Up until the last few years of my life I was a big beer drinker I enjoyed the taste of beer and being a gregarious type of person I enjoyed the bar company that went along with our daily happy hour session. We had our daily group of friends who were all characters themselves and then you get the passers by who have there own stories to tell to spice things up, some more exaggerated than others as the alcohol kicks in and everybody has a buzz on.

You meet your regulars, you meet strangers who are just moving into the community and trying to establish their social circle and then there's the odd nut from another town,

I loved the bar life, I learned so much about different people and the different walks of life and I felt a I had the education and personality to talk to a company executive on equal terms or a lavatory cleaner in their terms and still make comfortable conversation.

I was not an air's and graces type person anyway and even less so when I was in a bar, mingle with anyone I could, and mingle I did.

But there is a big dividing line between social drinking as I saw it, to the alcoholic state that I was soon to end up in. Once I thought that alcoholics were the down and outs who lay stupefied on park benches, dysfunctional and unable to work or communicate, but that wasn't ever going to be me or was it?

I thought I was too intelligent than that, I could give it up any time I wanted, so I thought, after all I didn't take drugs at all, that's what you get hooked on, no marijuana, (never even smoked a joint in my life, not one) no cocaine and no heroin, so the park bench wasn't even on my radar screen although clearly my alcohol intake was increasing steadily and people were talking about me. I had basically lost it.

The turning point for me was the introduction of wine into my daily drinking regimen, looking back this was a huge mistake as I really enjoyed it and became somewhat addicted, now I was drinking beer and wine in any order and large quantities of it too.

In midweek I would think nothing of 5 pints of beer at Happy Hour and then going home and having 4/5 large glasses of wine as a nightcap, this became a nightly ritual until the weekend when I got a bit more sporty and took even more.

I never once had a hangover, my body had adjusted to it and therefore there was no deterrent for me to stop.

Some colleagues who used to travel with me regularly on company business used to say when we got to the bar remember the one in three rule---one beer for every 3 he drinks he's got a bloody alcohol engine in his body and it never stops running.

My weekend drinking increased as well, I started drinking wine in the morning before I played golf on Saturday and Sunday each week, my excuse was "to relax myself, slow my swing down" and not be so jerky. And it worked, funny as it would seem for most, I did play much better golf that I did when I was sober and in fact managed to get my handicap down from a 9 to a 3 over 2 years. The guys I used to play with would greet me at the first tee at 9.30 in the morning and say "have you had your breakfast yet" knowing full well it wouldn't be ham and eggs, and I would reply, yep, 3 glasses of wine and a cigar. They used to chuckle at that, probably thought that I was exaggerating, but there wasn't any ham and eggs for me, just the wine and the cigar.

Drinking to this extent believe it or not did not affect the quality of my business performance at work for I had always drummed it into myself over the years always, always, take care of business and everything else will fall into place. And I apparently did, as I received performance rewards year after year and felt content that I was doing a good job, no danger of losing it, but I did admit to myself privately that the excessive drinking was starting to make me make bad decisions in both my personal life and my business life and as you read on you'll see why.

I was starting to lose track of household bills and my bank accounts and had taken on more credit cards against my better judgment, I was a man steadily going out of control and I realize now that I should have sought professional evaluation or counseling help, but I didn't, I let the runaway train continue, it was scary for me but evidently unstoppable, even as hard as I tried to reduce my alcohol consumption I couldn't do it.

I used to joke with my golfing friends "great party last night guys, must have been really good for I got up and started shaving the mirror instead of my face" ---but maybe it wasn't a joke, maybe I really did this?

Eventually after years of drinking like this I realized I was On the Slide, on one of these Helter Skelters that you get at the Fair where you start at the top and spiral slide your way down to the bottom, and just like all slides, the bottom sure comes quick and hard, I was there before I knew it.

It was time for the alcohol and substance and abuse Therapist, my wife had told me time and time again to make an appointment but since I thought I already knew what the outcome would be and not being willing to face up to the AA classes and the other stuff I had put it off and put it off many times. This time it was for real, I knew I had to have help and set up an appointment with a well known and experienced Therapist, Mr. Larry Watkins.

It didn't take me long to find out that this guy was a brilliantly experienced professional, he was in his mid fifties and had seen it all, the denials, the lies, the misconceptions. In my case I was going to tell him the exact truth, no playing it up or playing down, it will be what it will be. I have always taken the view point that if you go see a doctor you have to be totally truthful and whatever advice he prescribes you must at least try it and give it a chance.

After an hour of honest questions and answers with Mr. Watkins he summarized his diagnosis and referenced some big medical book on his shelf that he could recite from about substance behavior and their symptoms "Mr. Wylie you are indeed an alcoholic as far as alcoholics go, your body has acquired an incredible tolerance for alcohol and it is my recommendation that you go to a Detox in-patient program and try to reach total abstinence". However, with your cultural background I don't think that you will want to give up altogether nor do I think you could you do it anyway even if you tried.

During the course of our Therapy session, Mr. Wylie, I noticed that you moved your legs in the chair about 50 times, so clearly you are very hyperactive and need some medicine to calm you down. With this medicine it will be okay to have a few drinks but only a few otherwise you will be in the same situation as before, you will also have to have more willpower to combat the urge for drinking wine, the medicine I have given you will not help if you continue to drink as much as you do . I took the Therapist's advice very seriously and acted upon it immediately, the wine was over but the damage was already done, it was too late as you'll see in the following chapters of this book.

I wish I had seen the Therapist earlier.

Chapter Eight

Suburban Blues

Several years later—January 2007, Happy New Year! The year took off with a bang, yeah a big bang alright, the 5.7 liter engine on my 1998 Chevy Suburban blew up on the way to work January 4, cracked cylinder block, seemed to be a common fault according to the dealer that I got it towed to . As I was pitifully looking at the steam coming out the engine block and radiator, the dealer callously looked at me and said calmly," No problem, Sir, we can put a rebuilt engine in it, it'll only cost $4,000, there is a guy up the road who specializes in this, he'll have it done right away." Four-thousand dollars I said, fucking ridiculous I've just paid $800 dollars for a new radiator and now this happens, what a disastrous start to the New Year.

The dealer once again mentioned casually, "Well, it's $4,000, but it's like a new engine, 3-year warranty, you won't get a better deal." At this point I was thinking inwardly to myself, $4,000, the truck's seven years old and it's hardly worth seven thousand dollars in total when in good shape, and there are other nagging issues that needed to be fixed anyway, like squeaking breaks, rubbing wind shield wipers and also the huge tires, the size of wagon wheels were starting to look bare. "

Fuck me!" I said out loud. "Four-thousand dollars, eh?" I said dwelling on it again, then the crafty dealer put the boot in, "Well, Mr. Wylie, I can make you an offer for the whole truck, we will repair it, rebuild it and sell it. Then he rubbed it in, "we have specialists who only work on these rebuilds you know?" How much do you think it's worth, he says curiously, just as I was thinking it's worth about $5 dollars max, I spluttered $1500 dollars. "No, No", Mr. Wylie, the crafty dealer said, "I was thinking maybe $700 - $800 dollars. I know how to play this Moroccan bartering game I said to myself, so I replied "I thought I was giving it away to you at $1500, I was hoping for more like $2000". The crafty dealer retorted "$1000, final offer", Oh! Fuck! I had to make an instant decision or I might have to take the lame duck back with me and start all over again.

"Deal" I cried out to the crafty dealer, I put my hand forward to shake on the deal and of course he duly obliged, the lame duck was gone, the only car that I had ever paid off in my life and the one that I really enjoyed driving the most, was now history.

Now I have no wheels and a bad credit rating which will make it difficult to buy another car and have manageable payments – what a start to the New Year, 2007, but little did I know this was only the "start".

I reflected on my 2001 DUI as I walked through the parking lot and thought about all the promises I had made to my wife and myself about cutting down on the drinking, now I began to realize, too late as usual, that I'd got worse instead of better, my finances were in a mess, my relationship with my wife and family was strained to the max and now I had another car problem to face up to. I, the one that could have easily afforded a brand new Jaguar if I'd just moderated my lifestyle, one who had the vision of a brand new Jaguar sitting there with the keys dangling waiting for me to open it, then I looked back to see the 1998 lame duck getting towed away.

Every little boy in Scotland's dream of owning a Jaguar was now history, far out of reach, never to be seen again. I was disgusted

54

with myself.

The drinking has ruined you I thought to myself, wish I'd never started on it, look at the mess I'm in now, behind in my mortgage payments, credit card loans and other debts up the ying yang, yeah for me the American Dream was becoming the American Nightmare, Stephen King or Vincent Price couldn't have done a better job of scaring me, as much as I was scaring myself.

Oh, well, just get on with it, it could be worse you could be a crack head or a heroin addict, they're the ones that end up with nothing, stealing to keep their habit going or standing at the exit to the highway with a cardboard sign "will work for food ", food my ass, the only food they wanted was their next 2 minute highs. This wasn't going to be me, I only drink wine and beer don't I?

Fuckin' wrong again!, for in reality, the park benches were exactly where I was heading, the only thing that would maybe stop me were the pensions I was due from the company in Scotland and the one in USA, total of $2800 a month, this was my safety net if all else failed, so I convinced myself that I had nothing to worry about, I was still safe with my little safety net. I re-assured myself that I was not going down the drain, no way, stop being negative, cut down on the drinking, get new wheels and get it on with it, it'll all work out, you'll see.

As I stood in the low class dealer's parking lot looking for my next new car, a golfing buddy who worked there approached me," hey John, haven't seen your lame duck parked in your driveway, I know you need a new car, so let's get going. It was pissing down of rain that night but that didn't worry my buddy, Frankie, out popped the umbrella and off we went. Surely Frankie , my golfing buddy would not be like the crafty dealer, he wouldn't do that to his old friend, would he?, Twenty minutes later in the pissing rain and in the dark , he was trying to sell me a 3rd world country SUV, yes a foreign piece of shit for $26,000, he was starting to make the crafty dealer look like Little Red Riding Hood, yes he was the Wolfe alright, he wanted the deal, golfing buddy or no golfing buddy he wanted the deal right there, without any of the slightest bit of conscience coming into it. The rain got heavier and heavier and after 3 Skoda SUV's I gave up and told him sympathetically, sorry Frankie, I haven't seen anything I like, you'll need to find something better or I'll have to go elsewhere.

The very next morning at 8.00 am at work, I had hardly taken a sip out of my coffee when I got a phone call saying that a gentleman (the Wolfe) called Frankie was waiting outside in the lobby for me.

As I walked to the lobby I thought not another Skoda I hope, but when I got to the entrance I was impressed to see Frankie standing next to a big beautiful top of the range GMC Yukon, dark grey with silver trim washed and polished to the hilt, gleaming in the morning sunshine.

Frankie greeted me, "I know you didn't like those little cracker boxes I showed you last night, not the right type of car for a man of your status, this is the right car for you the Wolfe said, here's the keys, let's go for a spin, big boy!

A spin we did and the Wolfe had got me, it was comfortable, had all the bells and whistles, heated seats, classy sound system, it had it all, all I needed to do now was sign the papers and I would be driving a dream car again.

The Wolfe started the payments off at $700 a month, I said "come on Frankie I'm your golfing buddy if I have to make that payment there'll be no money left in the kitty to play golf with you " .

After much deliberation and to-ing and fro-ing to the sales manager's office which is the usual car dealer's trick, we got the payment down as Frankie would call it to " a mere $535 a month " over six years, yes six fuckin, years, but considering my bad credit, and circumstances, I jumped all over it, the papers were signed and I had nice wheels again and another 26,000 dollars worth of debt wrapped round my neck, another nail in the debt coffin lid, but nice wheels, eh?

Once through January and February, life was good, I still visited the bar every night for the happy hour just like Cheers, then a few big glasses of wine for a night cap when I got home, this routine continuing as previous years.

Chapter Nine
Daytona Bike Week

Then March came-----

I was talking to an old friend of mine, Alex from Scotland, who reminded me that Daytona Bike Week was taking place in the second week of March in Florida, we'd both been there 10 years before and had one of the biggest blasts ever in our partying career. So I invited he and his girlfriend (who incidentally was a sex therapist) over for the party of all parties. For most folks Bike Week conjures up the thoughts of Hell's Angels riding their Harleys down main street with a joint in their hands with their biker girls sitting in the back seat flashing their biker girl titties to everyone and all.

The fact of the matter is, yes, Bike Week is mostly like that, but there are also a lot of doctors, lawyers, teachers and other professionals who love to participate in this event, throwing off their professional mantles for a week of sheer anonymous madness.

At the official start of Bike Week with 250,000 bikers lined up in Main Street ready to go, the roar of the engines is earth shattering, a thunderous roar from hell, just fitting for the Hell's Angels that ride them.

There are all shapes and sizes of people and bikes there, most biker guys looked like gorilla's with their masses of chest hair sticking out of their black leather vests, their biker girls revealing cleavage showing like the Grand Canyon----- and mostly everyone wore a bandana, this and the leather chaps and boots they wore, were indicative of the free spirit of America where dress does not maketh the man.

Our favorite pub was located in New Smyrna Beach, it was called Pub 44, there was a huge Marquee set up in the grounds and rock bands played from 1.00 p.m. to 4.00 a.m., most them stoned out of their minds along with the audiences they were playing to. The atmosphere and the sights were phenomenal, the focus was on having the maximum fun you could have---- maximum

There were all sorts of competitions to participate in, there was the biggest ass competition and believe me some of the participant's asses made an elephants ass look like a newborn baby's. The biggest belly competition was the same, the woman that won looked like she was 9months pregnant but was in fact not.

In the most pierced and tattooed part of the body contest, one guy pulled up the inside of his big lips and it read in big blue letters tattooed on the inside "dicks are for chicks", but he didn't win funny as it was, there were bodies where not one square millimeter of bare flesh could be seen, due to the overwhelming number of tattoos imprinted on their body. Some were disgustingly ugly, some were erotically attractive but tattoos are like bandanas, ------ the Harley Rider's theme signature.

After 2 nights of partying craziness at the PUB 44, we headed out to the Cabbage Patch Pub in the country. This place is infamous for nude biker girls wrestling in coleslaw in a boxing ring and sure enough when we got near the parking lot we could see that the cars had overflowed into the street and we ended up having to park about a mile from the pub and walk the remainder.

Who would have thought that such a crowd would come to watch 2 nude biker bitches face off in a boxing ring full of coleslaw? But the level of normality for these biker folks is not anything you've ever imagined, in fact, with them, normality doesn't exist, it's full blown eccentric craziness 24/7, or forever----- until death.

After 4 days of biker mania, we headed to Gulfstream Park thoroughbred horseracing, thinking of course that some of the money we spent partying in Daytona would be recovered, so we emptied out one of the suitcases with the expectation that we would bring it back full of money----**Fuckin' wrong again!** Seems that horseracing tracks are not a layman's way of making money, in fact it's the exact opposite, if you bet in each race the odds are overwhelmingly in favor of the track and it didn't take me long to find this out, bet on every race I did with zero returns

After 9 races out of 10, meticulously studying the form, we had lost our ass and Alex took a photograph of me with a racing form ready to stuff it up my asshole.

Not giving into losing we decided to try another tactic, we took the 10th race runners and cut out the numbers, put them in a hat, then selected 3 blindfold---the rest you've already have assumed, yes, we picked the first 3 in race 10 and recouped our money, congratulating ourselves on the way back to the hotel on the brilliance of our tactical change in picking the winners. The remainder of the night I don't remember.

Soon it was time to take Alex and the sex therapist back to Orlando, the vacation was over quicker than a lighting bolt it seemed and soon they would be flying over the pond to London and we would be heading back to North Carolina, a stinkin' rotten 10 hour drive in 90-100 heat.

Alex told me later that they got loaded at Orlando Airport and bought Mr. and Mrs. mouse ears and put them on as they headed to the check in and security.

At the check in the clerk politely asked "and what name are we booked in under "Can't you see, I thought it would be obvious says Alex?" The clerk looked at them with a strange look in her face that questioned Alex's remark, "our tickets are booked under Mr. and Mrs. Mouse says Alex", the clerk grunted and clearly wasn't happy, they were lucky to get their tickets and not their real ears chopped off never mind Minnie's!

There was another little incident at the security check in, Bonnie the Sex therapist who was now as drunk as hell was screaming at the TSA guys to be strip searched rather than the normal screening and this caused a lot of commotion. This outlandish behavior would probably have been okay as a joke maybe in less sensitive parts of the world but not in Orlando, they didn't see it like that and Bonnie was warned to follow the normal process or risk getting ejected. She reluctantly got screened without the feel of a masculine pleasure of a TSA screener's hands

Next thing we know is, Alex and Bonnie were winging it across the Atlantic and we were back in North Carolina.

I had puked and shit all the ten hours back from Daytona, the journey taking 13 hours instead of the ten planned and I did not make it back to work until the Wednesday, 2 days later .

Fuckin' great trip Daytona, can't wait for next year! Yeah?

Chapter Ten

Going Down the Drain

Our bank account had been hammered with the Florida trip, now down another $4500, since we'd gone unwittingly to Florida in the college spring break when all the prices were jacked up at least twofold due to the influx of rich college kids. It was hard to get a decent hotel anywhere for under $300.

Bloody expensive week, we said, bloody expensive as we headed to the dog kennel to pick up our 6 months old beautiful wiemeranner puppy dog called Maggie, she was happy to see us and nearly bowled us over as we collected her at the kennel door.

"Great to see you Maggie' exclaimed my wife," good puppy dog, you're so beautiful".

Well she wasn't so beautiful the following week, because she took sick and we found out from the vet that she'd swallowed an old corn on the cob that had been buried in the backyard. The cob was stuck firmly in the dog's intestines and could only be removed by open surgery. This was when we discovered that the Health Care System in America for pets is the same as for humans, idiotically overpriced and unaffordable to most ordinary folks, but, nevertheless, Maggie was priceless to us, " go ahead Mr. vet and do what you have to do to save her, we'll worry about the $1,500 surgery price tag later.

Maggie recovered quicker than our wallets did, as she belted at full speed around the backyard, we wondered how we were going to face the $1500 bill along with all the other debts incurred from our trip to Daytona and the broken suburban.

Surely things can only get better in 2008? Fuckin' wrong again!

It was my wife's birthday on April 5, she was a young 62 and we decided to go to the old traditional Plantation House restaurant called the Legacy out in the country, expensive but elegant dining, great menu and exquisite ambience, couldn't really afford it but what the hell, she's never going to be 62 again.

We had a fantastic meal and birthday night until ill fate was bestowed on us once again. The Legacy is set in beautiful gardens front and rear and my wife, Sadie, loves flowers and all garden plants, so it was natural for her to leave the table after the meal and go look at the gardens.

As she stepped towards the balcony stairs I heard this awful thump followed by loud screams from the other restaurant patrons and I looked up to see my wife lying on the balcony stairs leading down to the gardens. She was bleeding profusely from her mouth and head and I could see that she was badly dazed.

We gently picked her up as all the other patrons looked on in disbelief to see this once elegantly dressed and joyful birthday person now saturated in blood and being carried out hanging to each of our arms like a ventriloquist's dummy.

We took her to the hospital emergency room where she had an x-ray and was diagnosed with severe concussion, a split lip, and her 2 front teeth knocked out and the adjacent 2 damaged. She was devastated, it's bad enough for a man to have no front teeth but for a woman it's even more traumatic, and traumatic for her it was. It was even more traumatic however when we got to the dentist as you will see as you read on.

Sadie was up at the crack of dawn the next day, a rare occurrence, rummaging through the yellow pages looking for a Periodontist, and we were lucky to find one that could take her that day and save her dignity. She wasn't going to walk around toothless no matter what.

I was pleased that she'd found somebody that could give her treatment the same day but at the same time I knew that Periodontists don't come cheap as I'd had gum disease treatment earlier in the year that cost $ 3,000 so I couldn't imagine what it would cost for 2 new front teeth and repairs to the adjacent 2. I was soon to find out, the cost would be $ 8,000 just for the 2 front teeth, 50% had to be paid up front or no treatment, now why do you think that was? --- I'll tell you, nobody can afford these exorbitant dental costs therefore the dentists know if they don't get paid up front they'll never get the remainder of the money. No way, so you have to pay up front

My wife proceeded to get her teeth fixed, and she was happy, very happy, smiling all the way home with her new choppers, but whilst I was happy about her restored appearance I wasn't smiling about the bill, $4,000 up front and the other $4,000 payable over the next 2 years.

It goes without saying that if dentists in America keep on charging these ridiculous prices there will only be one result----the majority of Americans in the next ten years or sooner will be toothless and gumsy or wearing the full "U" as they call dentures in New York or falsers as they call them in Scotland. Now I make light of this but it will become a serious embarrassment in the U.S.A. in years to come if indeed it isn't already happening, nice teeth will be a thing of the past, one lone tooth might be the norm for most ordinary folks. Dentistry will only be for the rich and famous.

So now we're only in the beginning of April, and so far we've had the truck engine blow up, the dog's surgery, the spring week robbery and the wife's teeth knocked out followed my gum disease, 2007 will long be remembered by the Wylie's.

"That's it" I said, nothing else can possibly happen, we've got our year's worth of misfortune in four months, rest of the year should be okay---**Fuckin' wrong again!**

No sooner had I got my $3,000 lump sum performance award at work, when the washing machine and the dryer blew up within one week of each other so most of the lump sum went to replacing these units and other bills----sound familiar? The performance award was killed outright and so were our already beleaguered finances, can't get a break at anything. I thought, bring in 2008 now, right now!

Chapter Eleven
Snippets from Japan Trip

However, there was some good news on the horizon , my bi-annual trip to Japan was coming up and I was excited at the thought of a company expenses paid trip that would let me escape from all these other domestic financial nightmares.

Then I had another master plan, why don't I meet my Scottish friend Alex in Tokyo, after all, he would only have to pay his flight from Scotland and then I could hide him under my business expenses, the hotel room was paid for by the company anyway and I would be entertaining a lot of Japanese customers night after night so one more head count wouldn't matter would it?, not against the background of a 70 Million dollar contract, one wee extra meal a night and a few drinks surely wouldn't count would it? Okay the deal was on, called him right away and, yes, we were soon on our way to Tokyo, bloody Tokyo no less, not Chinatown D.C., Tokyo in the far east!

Now I 'm not going to dwell on our time spent in Japan, only to tell you some of the more spicy bits of the trip, the rest would be a book of it's own, believe me---a big book at that!

Also, I didn't know at the time that this trip was eventually going to be the final curtain for me in America, such is the mystery of life no one knows what's ahead, Destiny takes over and can kick you in the ass, and by the end of 2007 my ass had been kicked so hard it felt like a pin cushion.

So just a few snippets about Japan, a country of 150 million people crammed into an area the size of Rhode Island! If you want some space from your neighbors, forget it, they're right beside you, like it or not. There are no open spaces in Japan, zero.

I've traveled there for more than 20 years so I know the culture very well but we'll stick to one subject that seems to be prevalent there--- SEX!

I don't know how many people know it but the Japanese wrote the sex book " Pillow Talk " so we'll concentrate on "Kibuchi Choi" which must be associated with Pillow Talk but I don't really know, what the hell do I know about the Japanese language, my Scottish Japanese ain't too good and their Japanese Scottish ain't good either.

However, every time we got a taxi in the Shinjuko area (like Soho in London) the taxi drivers would always mention Kibuchi Choi so we knew we had to try it and try it we did, first bloody night there.

It works like this; we thought it would be strip show but we were soon to learn different as we approached the little theater ahead of us. It did in fact start with a variety of gorgeous strippers, stripping tantalizing as only they know how, but I was not prepared for the next step in the Kibuchi Choi process, suddenly the lights dimmed sharply and without any warning the whole audience of Japanese men jumped up simultaneously and started to play the game that everyone used to play at school, Rock Breaks Scissors, Scissors Breaks Rock, Paper Covers Rock, this is the game you stand facing each other with your hands behind your back and then you release your hands simultaneously to show your choice.

We were still puzzled by this action but soon realized what was going on, yes the competitors were competing for their turn to have sex on the stage and even more fascinating for us, the ones that lost were totally pissed off at missing out.

The next thing I know the "winner's" are assembled in line on the stage awaiting their dream girl---all of the women on stage were European, American, British, Canadian, no Japanese, all had blonde hair which is a big attraction to Japanese men, as all the Japanese women have dark black hair, no exceptions., Blondes women are a scarcity and a great desire for them, a big fantasy, for what I saw in that theater was fierce competition, only blondes could have caused that.

The next sex stop was the $99 all you can drink blow-job bar ---yes you pay the $99 up front at the entrance and then you pick your woman of choice, they take you to a little private booth and ply you with as many beers as you want until you're ready for the blow, our strategy was to drink as much as we could on the basis that the blow job would be sustained longer, so naturally for me I had about six beers beforehand. I looked over at the other booth and my friend Alex had taken steps a bit further as he took the sixty nine position, mad bastard that he was. I tried to explain to him that you don't get tongue condoms but he was erotically charged and it was too late for such incidentals of the flesh.

All of a sudden the ten days in Japan were over, I was heading back to the U.S.A. and Alex was once again heading back to Scotland, another wild adventure over.

The tears were streaming down my face as we said our last goodbyes, he was headed to the economy class section and me, being the spoiled bastard that I was, I was heading to the Business Class V.I.P lounge, life was good, so I thought.

I returned from Japan feeling really good, we had been spoiled rotten living in the best hotels, wining and dining in top restaurants and enjoying the cultural experiences. The business meetings had also gone incredibly well with promises of future joint ventures for years to come.

Chapter Twelve
The Unaffordable Hypochondriac Wife

J ust as I was reminiscing about the good times in Japan, unknown to me there was another disaster looming up right on my doorstep, for no sooner had I got back from Japan and stepped into the doorway of the house when my wife told me she'd been having problems with her motor control and had experienced incontinence. I could see that she was very upset and being an RN herself she had a good idea of the gravity and complexity of the problems ahead. I didn't know what to expect but whatever it was there would naturally be more medical expenses involved and this prospect was frightening me just as much as the medical condition itself.

Where does one start with all this? The neurologist first examined by wife by checking her basic motor controls and his initial diagnosis from past experience suggested that she may have brain tumor. Further MRI and lab tests however showed up negative, there was no tumor just some slight lesions of the brain but none that could cause the conditions she was having.

Several other costly tests were now performed, in these circumstances of diagnostic inconclusiveness the doctor's check every disease possible and determine the cause by a process of elimination. The top potentials. Multiple Sclerosis---negative, Limes disease –negative, Brain Cancer---negative

But my wife is a known Hypochondriac I thought to myself, she has so many pills in her medicine cabinet that when CVS or Rite Aid run out they call her up for a top up. So with all these expensive medical tests going on all showing up negative, my layman diagnosis was starting to tend towards a blind boil on her ass that was causing all the problems, my hunch was right because at the end of the day there were no major diseases diagnosed, the only disease she had was that of a Hypochondriac's mind, an expensive mind in America that no-one could possibly afford. Now I don't want to get into the pro's and con's of the American Health Care System but I do think that Americans are brain washed into thinking that they have the best system in the world---just wait until you have a serious illness and see if you think the same.

I think not but I'll leave you to decide.

I guess as a European my biggest gripe is that I pay proper health insurance so why shouldn't it cover everything in total, why do I have $1500 deductibles, $ 30-$50 co-pays, 20% hospital payments and so on. If I'm making $120,000 a year which is apparently in the top 20% earners in the U.S.A. how can the average American afford these medical bills, they can't of course that's why the system is unworkable, even bazaar in my view and the majority of American's think the same way ----or maybe they don't ----until they have a serious medical problem that is.

Four months went by with my wife not working, no income coming in and both of us up to our eyeballs in debt, mortgage arrears, loans, credit cards, medical bills, they were all closing in on me and I knew it, but it was like a train coming at you at full speed and somehow it couldn't be stopped.

Chapter Thirteen
The American Dream Blown?

*N*ow came the Coup de Graz, I felt like a Matador that had lost to the bull, tossed up in the air and gored to death, the end of the American dream was near and I knew it, when you're in such drastic circumstances, your instinct tells you what's coming next and it starts with the letter 'D', yes, Doom, bloody Doom.

And Doom it was, I went into the office as usual on November 17 just before Thanksgiving and got a message on my voicemail from the HR manager (and believe it or not her name was Tammy Wolfe, what an irony!), "John I'd like to ask you a few questions, just pop into my office at 1.00pm and we'll take it from there".

I was suspicious right away because I'd been with the company 12 years and hadn't had a single direct call from HR. My instinct told me once again that she wasn't calling me to come collect my Thanksgiving turkey so I knew it would be something else and not good at that. And not good it was--- she made it sound so casual, just a few questions, but in fact when I got to her office, there was a conference call arranged with Global Security as if I was some sort of criminal who had screwed the company for the last 12 years that I worked there.

"We would like to ask you some questions about the use of your Corporate American Express Card , there are some anomalies that we need clarification on said the global security man

"Now I see that you have some supermarket charges on your card, was that personal or for business purposes, of course he already knew the answer, how could I possibly have said that the supermarket charges were not personal, should I have said I bought some steaks for my customers and cooked them at the efficiency room in their hotel---no don't think that would fly so I answered honestly "personal charges". Mr. Wylie, he replied, you know this is a violation of company policy, don't you?

Yes, I said hesitantly because I knew where this was going and it wasn't going to be in my favor that's for sure. "Then Mr. Wylie on this date and that date, you withdrew cash from the ATM using your company American Express card, was this business or personal use---maybe I should have said business again but how could I have upheld drawing out $1,000 here and there with no customers and no customer receipts---I was going down quickly and knew it. The reality was that I had withdrawn this money to pay the bills while my Hypochondriac wife was off work for 4 months and the all the medical and other bills were flooding in, what was one to do? I had no option except bankruptcy.

Personal use of your American Express card is a violation of Corporate Policies----blah, blah, blah, the investigator crowed.

Now Mr. Wylie, let's talk about your Japanese expenses and then he proceeded to review every single receipt going back over the last two visits, a period of 13 months in total, he began asking about specific receipts I had submitted.

Mr. Wylie you have a receipt for $600 for the White Elephant and another for the same amount in Pub Abscontia and they are not itemized receipts like I would expect they are just summary receipts, why are they not itemized as they normally are? Dead easy pal I said, ever been to Japan yourself where it's $8-$10 for one pint of beer and a decent Western meal in Tokyo can cost you on average $150, that how much it cost in Japan, so these receipts are in no way unreasonable, it's just the way it is there. These receipts are normal I said knowing that they had been padded, I then tried to mitigate the circumstances" "any time I've gone to Japan in the past it's cost me a lot of personal money, you can go to a Karaoke hostess bar for example, forty dollars an hour per person plus drinks, then you have to pay 5 dollars for each song you sing whether you're a good singer or a lousy one like me. So $600 is nothing, when the Japanese go out this is what they expect to spend, they don't go out very much but when they do they accept that this is going to be the cost, this is what it is like, like it or not.

There was a dead silence at the other end of the line. I could sense that the investigator wasn't buying my excuse as plausible as it was, for anyone who has visited Japan knows how ridiculously expensive it is.

The investigator then asked pointedly, "how many people traveled with you", innocently; I replied "one company employee and one customer."

"Oh really Mr. Wylie, what about Mr. Alex McFarlane, who was he, he's on the hotel bill that you submitted for the Keio Plaza in Tokyo."

Mr. McFarlane paid his own way I replied, the only advantage for him joining me was the use of the hotel as a base which would be paid for by the company anyway whether he was there or not so there should be no issue. I knew the next question that was coming, did Mr. McFarlane travel throughout Japan with you, asked the investigator? Yes, I admitted, knowing that I had charged Alex's weekly Japan rail pass ($ 360) to my company American Express card. I was now unmistakably caught with expense "anomalies" and that together with the dodgy receipts and the personal use of the card put the lid on it. I was done and I knew it, no escape, I'm going down. The call with the investigator ended and the HR manager said "John, you've been a great asset to this company; we'll try and get it sorted out for you."

Sorted out I thought, even the great man himself Houdini couldn't get out of this one!---and I was right, once the investigators smell your blood they're like hounds on the trail, every little detail was scrutinized thereafter while I was on suspended leave for two weeks. I knew it looked really bad on paper to someone who didn't know me so I knew there was only one outcome and I was right --- termination.

After 2 two weeks of deliberation, the HR manager called me up and cheerily asked me to come to a meeting on the Monday morning at 9.00 am. She seemed to give me hope that I would still be employed and just get a warning, there was nothing said like that, but the tone of her voice suggested it.

I went to the meeting nervous as a whore in church but with a glimmer of hope that I might get a slap on the wrist and that would be it---**Fuckin' wrong again!**

At the meeting my manager who was more nervous than me told me that he had no option but to terminate me, he seemed to be truly apologetic "didn't want to do this but have no option, it's a corporate decision that can't be revoked". I then shakily signed the exit papers and 12 years of good standing with the company was gone in a flash and I was now officially Down the Drain, well and truly, had it as they say. At age 58 I felt like a skeptical old age pensioner on the market for a new job, with a pessimistic attitude.

The American Dream seemed to be completely shattered and the nightmare started-----but that old saying "what will be will be" rang through my head as I headed home to give the wife the bad news.

If you believe in destiny, which I do, read on, I am not a deeply religious person but I do believe that things happen for a reason and the subsequent events left me in awe.

Chapter Fourteen

The Detox Experience

I think it was one of Newton's laws that says "what goes up must come down", so the reverse logic for me was "what goes down should go up" therefore it was my objective to climb back up out of this horrible mess I was now in, the question for me was " how do I do it, I'd lived this way for nearly forty years", I know I've got pills from the doctor that helps but I'm still drinking on top of them although a bit more moderately-------until.

It was Christmas Eve in North Carolina and the weather forecast was 65 degrees, perfect weather for golf I thought so I called up the boys and arranged a tee time for 10.00 am. I made the big mistake of telling the wife that I would be back at 3.00 p.m. cause she's very strict on punctuality and I was not very good at living up to my commitments, somehow I always got distracted and turned up late to a growling wife. This time, as it turned out, was not going to be any different.

As usual, I took my cooler with twelve beers in it and I could top up as necessary at the 9th hole at the clubhouse, I didn't have any wine beforehand so I thought that was a positive sign of me trying to make progress on the alcohol reduction program. I was feeling good about that, but it wasn't to last long.

Our game finished about 2.30 p.m. but instead of going straight home as promised, I felt hungry and headed on my own to the seafood restaurant a mile down the road with crab stuffed mushrooms and a glass of Chardonnay firmly embedded in my mind, it'll only take about an hour I thought so the wife shouldn't be too grumpy if I'm just a little bit late, should she? **Fuckin' wrong again!**

The restaurant was packed due to the holiday shoppers and it took double the normal time for my stuffed mushrooms to arrive and meanwhile I was downing the Chardonnay's good style.

I left the restaurant at about 5 o'clock having downed about 5 glasses of wine along with the beers I'd already had on the golf course. I was now plastered and knew there would be trouble when I got home, but I was not expecting what was to come next, I thought I'd be able to smooth it over with the wife and that would be that----not so. When I opened the front door I was met with a wild animal with gnashing teeth and eyes of fury, the wife had had enough this time, this was the end for her, all the excuses and white lies weren't going to fly this time. I was done for.

She let loose with a verbal barrage of swearwords that would have made Snowhite look like a witch

She then picked up the phone and dialed 911 and said that I was threatening to kill her which was a complete lie which in turn caused me to go berserk and on the spur of the moment I grabbed her momentarily by the shoulders and pushed her across the kitchen counter. I then realized what I was doing and retreated quickly to the bedroom and locked the door and fell asleep.

I was awakened shortly thereafter by a loud knock at the bedroom door and a gruff voice calling for me to come out, "we are the Rocky Mount police and we need to talk to you".

I knew it was hopeless to try to fight this off and meekly withdrew myself from the room.

The cop explained that my wife had signed papers to have me committed to detox and that charges had been pressed for grabbing her the way I did. I tried to explain how she had provoked me with her threatening to kill lie, but it was hopeless, seems like in all these domestic violence cases, it's the man of the house that get's locked up no matter what.

Next thing I knew the bracelets were on me and I was sat in the back of the police car heading to the local general hospital for evaluation.

I put my gurney on and sat in the bed watching TV until the doctor came to see me and after examining me he said you need to go to detox for a minimum stay of 72 hours. I found out later this is state law when you are committed involuntary, you have to do 72 hours before you're allowed out of the detox center mainly because it takes this amount of time to get free of any alcohol or other substances in your body.

The detox center next to the general hospital in Rocky Mount was full, so I was taken by the police in handcuffs to the center in Greenville about a 45 minute ride away. It felt like the longest ride I'd ever had, it was 3.00 a.m. in the morning, the handcuffs were killing me and I just wanted to get to the hospital and get it over and done with.

But the hospital that I expected to be admitted to was not what I had in mind, I was expecting it to be like the hospital I'd just left, private room, T.V twenty four hours a day, attentive nurses and good food.

The detox center was just like jail, it was a lock down facility where anyone admitted cannot leave without authorization. Everyone had to wear the same scrubs, not quite an orange jumpsuit like jail, but very similar, same with the slippers and green socks that everyone else wore. This in itself felt humiliating to me but maybe that was part of the shock treatment, I could see that this was not going to be the rehab place that I had envisioned, I was expecting group therapy, recreational programs and more medication to get me off my alcohol addiction. Then again I wasn't a movie star either.

The admission started with three vials of blood taken from my arm and a needle prick to test for tuberculosis. I was then given 2 valium pills and ushered to my room. The room was bare and dismal looking, and as I walked in I could see that I had company, another guy was already snoring loudly and clearly out of it in the bed next to mine, I was to find out later his name was Elvis and he had overdosed on Heroin. I couldn't sleep that night, my immediate thoughts were to take revenge on my wife and her nutcase daughter for putting me in there, I could smash their cars during the night, I could move all my belongings out the house and leave them with a mortgage they had no chance of paying. These evil thoughts went through my mind as I stomped up and down the locked corridors of the detox center.

Medication distribution took place four times a day 6.00am, 1.00pm, 6.00pm and 9.00pm, each person being prescribed different medications according to their addiction. In my case it was valium and vitamin pills and after a couple of sessions I was feeling much better and more focused, the evil thoughts I'd had previously had were now wearing off and my concentration was on getting better and leaving this place at the earliest opportunity.

Breakfast was at 7.15 a.m. and when I entered the dining room it was a pitiful sight, most of the other patients were in there because of addiction to crack cocaine, heroin, pain pills, marijuana and other substances. My roommate, Elvis, who was 36 years old and 6ft 5in was definitely the worst affected, he was walking about like a zombie, no idea where he was and then I was told he was given the drug Thazirone which makes you ultra lethargic, walking in tiny steps like a toddler taking his first walk. Elvis scared me at first because he looked schizophrenic and I was frightened for my safety but as the heroin wore off and the Tharizone kicked in I started to talk to him and although he didn't look capable of any type of communication he did start to tell me about his issues and seemed to have some intelligence despite his out of it appearance.

He had been a heroin addict since he was thirteen and his arms and hands were riddled with needle holes, even down to his knuckles. He told me he was on disability and clearly to me he was dysfunctional and probably unemployable. I felt sorry for him and tried to help him with his meals that he couldn't even eat by himself. His degree of hopelessness had a profound effect on me, there was no way out for him, this was how he would live the rest of his life, in and out of institutions.

The story was mostly the same for the other men and women who were hooked on Heroin, one of the women who was 20 years old and a stripper nicknamed "Baby Girl" a nice looking blonde with a nice figure, told me she made 2,000 dollars a week in Cocoa Beach Florida and was taking 60 oxycontin pain pills a day which absorbed most of her salary. She had been visiting her mother in North Carolina for Christmas and she committed her involuntarily to detox when she saw the state of her. After 3 days she was allowed out but I suspect she would be heading back to Florida to do the same old thing, she made it clear she wasn't interested in stopping. She seemed happy enough surprisingly to me and at least she was making the money to support her habit and by her own admission had a job where you party every day and get well paid for it.

She told me her strategy for bringing in the dollars was to tease a man all night with the belief that you really like him and you want to go home with him and after five or so twenty five dollars lap dances you dump his ass and move on to the next gullible victim and repeat the process.

Baby Girl was gone after three days, the heroin withdrawals had gone and she was as chirpy as she could be as she waved goodbye to all of us that remained. Most of the other heroin and cocaine addicts were a very different story, they had lost everything, their jobs, their possessions, they had no where to go and their best prospect was a halfway house if they could find the bus fare to get there.

Most had felonies and couldn't get employed anywhere except construction sites connected to the halfway house system which had strict rules. There were no smiles here like Babygirl when she left, it was fear and intrepidation, living in a shelter or a halfway house was their very best hope. As I looked around I thought to myself if it wasn't for your company pensions and family support, this could be you, left with nothing, no hope, once again this was a rude awakening for me.

There were three other men in for alcohol treatment like me, two were in their fifties like me and the other was a strapping thirty six year old who built houses for a living. His name was Garret and he came from Nag's Head at the east coast, his mother had brought him all the way from there a five hour ride in the middle of the night to the detox center in Greenville and you could see that he needed it. He looked hellish, disheveled and all, and he was covered in tattoos from head to toe, there didn't appear to be a bare spot anywhere.

After talking to Garrett for a while I realized he was a reasonably intelligent hard working guy that had gone over the top with alcohol just like me. He told me he was drinking a bottle of whisky a day and a case and a half of beer too. To make matters worse his girlfriend owned one of the bars near his house, another big temptation I'm sure.

He also told me that he could ride his bicycle in one direction and hit nine bars or go the other direction and hit 6 bars and that's what he did most nights after his work as a carpenter. He was like me initially, mad at his mother for bringing him there but also realizing that he had to cut down or he would end up with fatal liver disease.

I talked to him about his tattoos and he told me the hardest one he ever had was the one done on the head of his dick, he told me it took about 2 hours the pain was so excruciating, each time the needle was inserted he would let out a scream until he finally had the tattoo "mighty mouse" tattooed permanently on his dick end. I told him I had "Welcome to Mombassa, have a Happy Holiday tattooed on mine, but I don't think he believed me!

Garrett was on valium like me and the treatment was working, we were both feeling better and looking better after a couple of days.

There was another alcoholic who had lost his job 9 months previous and spent the whole day on the computer gambling on Texas hold 'em. He told me he would sit with a huge cooler full of beer on one side of the computer and a trash can at the other and drink beer and whisky all day long while his wife was at work. When she came in from work, the dishes would be piled high and she would say can you give me a hand to clean up and his reply would be " wait a minute I've got a good hand here" Needless to say his ass was also committed involuntary to detox by his wife.

Although the detox center was set up like a jail, the staff of doctors, psychiatrists, nurses assistants etc were very caring for the patients and that combined with the hopelessness of the people I saw in there made me realize that the drinking had to come to an end I had to target for absolute abstinence. I read the AA book which I used to laugh at, at one time, but was totally surprised how beneficial it was, a lot of the disaster stories were just a mirror image of me. I looked at the steps to addiction and I was there at the very last step, now it was time to climb out the drain and get back to being the successful businessman that I was accustomed to being.

I signed up for further intensive therapy courses in the evening and vowed that I would never take another alcohol drink at least for three months or more. At least I was trying it seemed.

I lasted the three months ---just.

Final Chapter
No Turning Back?

How many times have you heard you're mother and father say "have you learned your lesson" as my mother spanked me she used to say as she spanked me in rhythm "don't you do that again" but a spanking never did anything for me, it had to be a thrashing or no change that's just the way it was for me, so learning the lesson was a big challenge, what was a guy like me going to do?

Moderation is the key I thought, I had to get from extremism to moderation or my biggest fear would be realized and I would end up penniless, a situation that I had never experienced before and something I know I couldn't handle, no way, there was no doubt in my mind that I had to change but as we all know change is not easy, especially when you've enjoyed the good life as I had done for 30 years.

The first step in my change process was to go to the doctor and seek advice, before I knew it I was permanently on valium which surprisingly enough for me calmed me down considerably, it seemed like it was a good substitute for alcohol. I was starting to think straighter and acting more sensibly, the fog was clearing up and I was definitely seeing everything in a new light and kicking myself for getting into this unthinkable mess that I had now got myself into.

I updated my resume which I hadn't done for the 12 years I was employed with the same company, never thought there was a reason to do it, never thought that I would lose my job, never even crossed my mind, but now it was a reality. I was in deep, deep shit and knew it. I had to get out.

My resume looked really good and with 35 years experience in aerospace I expected to get hired fairly quickly but I was now 58 years old, father time was indeed against me but in the past every interview I went for I had gotten the job so I reflected on that and regained my lost confidence.

I had cut down on the partying dramatically, a fraction of what I used to do and was feeling better on a daily basis. Just as my first pension check started to arrive I had a friend in an aerospace company who called me and told me there was a position that was perfect for me and when I saw the job description I realized that this was an incredible fit for me. This is where destiny takes over and I could feel it in my inner soul, this was my chance to get up out of the drain and never, ever go back.

I was terrified of being interviewed, I hadn't been interviewed for so long, but I had to knuckle down as they say and get on with it, for me this was a no fail situation.

I was interviewed by seven people individually on the one day but it didn't seem like the pressure interviews I'd had previously in my career, it seemed they needed me more than I thought, and I was right, after 30 days of an agonizing wait it was confirmed that I got the job, not only that, they were offering $25,000 more than I expected, it was exhilarating I felt I was starting a new life, a second chance if you will, no blowing it this time.

At the time of finishing this book I have now been employed by the company for 7 months and it feels that I've been rejuvenated. But as I mentioned earlier, change is a big challenge for everyone particularly if you're set in your ways like I was.

A classic example is my wife of 5 years. When I first met her and visited her house I knew immediately that housekeeping was not her forte and I was the opposite, everything had to be neat and tidy and looking good as if it had never been lived in, kept my house, my cars and everything I owned the same way.

I found out when she moved in that she was never happier than when the beds were not made, dirty clothes were strewn all over the place, the dishes were piled up in the sink and the African Grey parrot shitting on them.

I was absolutely convinced that I could change this but as much as I tried she only improved a miniscule amount, yes she would have whirlwind days when the house was immaculate but despite the praise I gave her, 2-3 days later it was back where it was, looking like a Scud missile intended for a military target had hit our house square on!

The point of this story about my wife is that most people don't change dramatically, there may be small incremental changes but don't expect them to go from one extreme to the other, it isn't going to happen.

So back to my situation, my new focus in my new job was moderation in everything you do, but in trying to accomplish this, I recalled my impression of people who I knew lived a moderate lifestyle and always found them to be boring to say the least, always telling you about the how much savings they've got, never gone anywhere, never done anything, despite there proclaimed wealth never even left the United States, only read about other countries but never physically experienced it----sad, I have met so many people in U.S.A that will talk about their European heritage but won't visit their country of birth because they are too obsessed by their wealth that they can't bring themselves to do it, they'd rather watch their money growing than risk a nice vacation.

So what is the outcome for me, I am trying to be moderate but it is not in my blood, I know that I can only keep this up so long before the moderation will burst. I know sooner or later it's going to happen that I'll go on a bender of some sort and the moderation will be over, so there's no fitting end to this story, I may have to write volume 2! See you in a year's time for an update.

John

Final Final Chapter
Big Red and the Dead Prostitute

J ust when I thought my life had turned around and I was settled into my new aerospace job and doing well the unexpected happened, self inflicted of course.

My relationship with my wife and live in step daughter (Big Red) which will be explained later in this chapter had deteriorated to the point that I no longer wanted to come home from work every night instead I went straight to the bar after work spent two hours there with my cheers friends and then went for dinner returning to my games room upstairs where I lived alone like a cave man. I did this for three months but it was a very lonely existence, my stepdaughter whom I had taken care of for five years free of charge turned into a living nightmare.

I should have known better, her nick name ''Big Red'' originated from her three years as a stripper when I my met her mother my wife she talked about her and called her an ''exotic dancer'' she told me this when I met her and that big red was a pistol, she even seemed proud of it.

Big red was five foot ten inches tall with flowing red hair and drop dead gorgeous, she turned heads everywhere she went but I was soon to find out that looks are not what counts, it's the inner soul and the character of a person that matters, she was a classic example of this.

I never really new her upbringing background it how it caused her to be so depressed,, miserable, and vengeful, she could be so sweet one minute and then turn into a vicious, hateful person, in a nanosecond and it seemed to me that she was bi-polar and frightening when her mood changed this way.

When I first met Big Red she gave me the impression that she was a very intelligent woman that knew everything about everything but I was soon to find out that this was a front to disguise her real identity, she actually knew nothing about nothing, she had no academic qualifications, her mother gave her everything materialistic but I stumbled across an e-mail one day that she wrote to a friend saying that her mother never really displayed any affection for her. Her mother was too busy galavanting with other men.

Maybe this is why she ended up an exotic dancer to get false affection from the clients that go to such places, Rich men had such a desire for her body they would have paid anything to have sex with her.

But there is a old saying in Scotland or maybe it's universal ''you don't bite off the hand that feeds you ''yet she apparently could not grasp this concept,, sometimes she would become explosive and call me a useless alcoholic but would lie in her bed all day with her mother in the next room while I went to work and worked my balls off to support the household. I could never understand this, where I grew up in Scotland it was the opposite we wanted to help our parents financially and otherwise. It was not the case with Big Red

If you had asked her to write down the word give she would have written down take that's how self centered she was and selfish she was.

Big Red's mother on the other hand was extremely intelligent and generous person to the point she would go overboard to help someone in trouble whether it was financial help, spiritual help, or just comfort she would be there for you no matter what. And at any price. She was a registered nurse but she was a genius academically who had the ability to be a top class doctor, her knowledge of medicine and medical conditions was that good, her IQ would probably be in the highest Mensa ratings, but common sense, she had none, Forget it.

She was addicted to pills and doctors, I used to joke that when CVS ran out of pills they called her up for replenishment, this was almost true because we had a cabinet full of pills for every disease known to mankind.

My wife Sadie was a country girl , she told me she was looking for a pig farmer when she met me but I was the very opposite a city boy who was used to bars and night life and gambling and people atmosphere that country girls could never understand

I thought I could change her and she thought she could change me, but in reality most people never change much, they might for a little while and then they revert to the way they were. That's life.

As time went by, I became increasingly isolated and frustrated living upstairs alone, I was the one going into a hard days work every day, yet I got the blame for the financial mess we were in. It was reverse logic to me, I could not understand why they would not get off their ass and go to work like me.

This situation was totally unacceptable to me and that's when I realized I had to get out and find another life.

I frequented the local bar often and started to meet other women a lot younger than myself, which boosted my ego but I was still not happy and eventually I flipped my lid, when you get to the point when you think your being fair and nobody appreciates you then that's when it's over.
It was over for me and I knew it, now I am looking for a new

woman,, as always for me, it seems I can never get what a normal person gets, I guess I came from low class and it sticks and that's the type of woman that I ended up associating with, yes low class but there is a limit to low class and I eventually exceeded that, I met a black woman in the local bar her name was Kimberly Lesley Anne and I discovered later that she was a prostitute living her life in a run down shit hotel in the worst part of town

But being the generous and passionate person that I am, I befriended her and somehow became attached, I don't know to this day why but it happened but it did.

Home life was becoming unbearable and I had the urge to walk away from the incredible pressures I was experiencing, I had a Scottish friend Alex whom I had known for twenty years and he had just recently immigrated to Thailand we always kept in touch with each other we were bonded like blood brothers and missed each other when we were apart.

With my home life in the shitter I made a spontaneous decision to go and join him in Thailand and leave my broken life in America behind.

I booked a flight on the internet that day and then I was of to Bangkok, the same day that I booked a flight Kimberley Lesley Anne the black prostitute called me out of the blue and asked me to meet her.

I explained to her that I was going to Thailand and offered her a $150 to drive me in my car to Raleigh Durham airport which was about a seventy mile journey, she agreed and off we went.

We had a good night in the local hooters restaurant and then spent the night together in the Fairfield inn by Marriott, strangely enough at that time she asked me to write a book about her life as a call girl, l she had taken notes but needed them to be properly compiled into a book manuscript, I said I would do this for her.

Kimberley was no ordinary call girl, she was clever by call girl standards which surprised me immensely.

My focus, however, was to get to Raleigh Durham Airport and head straight to Thailand.

I had enough of the good life in the land of the free, it was time to leave, my gut feeling told me so.

I told Kimberley to drive my Chevrolet SUV back to Rocky Mount and leave the keys with the bartender at my local bar. I found out later that this did not happen, just as I was ready to head to the airport departure lounge a woman police officer approached me regarding my out of date license plate. I thought there and then that I was going to be arrested but instead of issuing a fine she gave me a warning I can only assume that she liked me because of my Scottish accent.

It was also significant that she noticed Kimberley Lesley Anne sitting in the driving seat and that I was saying my last goodbye heading for Thailand.

Okay now I am on my way to Bangkok to meet my Scottish friend of twenty years, the flight from La Guardia New York was 15hrs 30min and I was glad when the plane touched down and I disembarked, I knew this was the start of a new life for me, I left Bangkok and traveled 10 hrs to my friends house in a small village called Prasat in the south east of Thailand near the Cambodian border.

On arrival at my Scottish friend's house he welcomed me with his girlfriend Dow and to my surprise two lesbian who were staying there also.

Now I was in shock, but much more was to come I just did not know it at the time, but as always in my experience, fate kicks in and what's going to happen is going to happen, you have no control over it.

After I settled into the village of Prasat in Thailand I received a e-mail from the local police station in Rocky Mount North Carolina USA stating that Kimberley Lesley Anne, the prostitute I had befriended had been found dead in my SUV and although I was not a person of interest they wanted me to call them and explain the circumstances.

Kimberley had died by natural causes in my car, when my Scottish friend and I got the e-mail message from the Rocky Mount Police, we were in total disbelief.

Here was I a seasoned alcoholic still alive at the grand old age of 59, Kimberley on the other hand was 42 and did not do much as far as I could see, except sell her body to survive. Kimberley's death made me realize that life is totally unpredictable, you never know what's round the corner.

Who could have imagined getting a message about a dead prostitute found in your own car, it could only happen to me, John Wylie.

As I write this final chapter from Cambodia I was found wandering around in the capital city of Phenom Penh in my underpants and with my golf shoes on, the airline company had lost my luggage and it took a whole week to retrieve it. I fitted in well in Phnom Pen, al the farangs (Asian name for westerners) were all nutters so even in this condition I still didn't look out of place.

This is the end of the DUI story for the time being, look out for the next Wylie book about travels in South East Asia, it will blow your mind as it did mine.

The final message or the moral of this story, so to speak is "Don't let this happen to You." You can see the reasons why.

www.ingramcontent.com/pod-product-compliance
Lightning Source LLC
Chambersburg PA
CBHW060637290526
45793CB00001B/289